Tour of the Isle of Wight: The Drawings Taken and Engraved by J. Hassell. ... in Two Volumes. ..., Volume 2

John Hassell

TOUR

OF

THE ISLE OF WIGHT.

THE DRAWINGS TAKEN AND ENGRAVED

BY *J. HASSELL.*

DEDICATED, BY PERMISSION, TO

HIS ROYAL HIGHNESS

THE DUKE OF CLARENCE.

IN TWO VOLUMES,

see page 224

VOLUME THE FIRST.

I wish I had been with you to see the Isle of Wight. JOHNSON.

LONDON:

PRINTED BY JOHN JARVIS,;

FOR THOMAS HOOKHAM, IN NEW BOND-STREET.

MDCCXC.

TO HIS ROYAL HIGHNESS

THE

DUKE OF CLARENCE.

SIR,

ENCOURAGED by the honour your Royal Highness has done me in permitting your name to appear at the head of this Work, I trust my exertions to render it worthy of so exalted and illustrious a patronage, have not been totally unsuccessful. To raise to public notice a young and enterprizing Artist, was the principal motive that influenced me to undertake the Work. If the success should be such as to pave the way for his future advancement, I shall be happy; at the same time I shall ever retain a high sense

a 2

of

of the obligation your Royal Highness has con-
fered upon me, by thus honouring the Work with
your patronage.

I am,

with profound respect,

YOUR ROYAL HIGHNESS'S

most obliged, most obedient,

and very humble servant,

T. HOOKHAM.

New Bond-street,
May 1st, 1790.

INTRO-

INTRODUCTION.

FROM a Tour of this kind, in which the
beauties of Nature are the object of our search,
we experience a pleasure that few other amuse-
ments can furnish. — The picturesque views,
which at every step present themselves to an
observant eye, while they pass unnoticed by the
plodding or hasty paffenger, afford the sentimental one a fund of entertainment, which at
once delights and improves the mind.

Almost every division of the kingdom in which
we have the happiness to live (we term it *happiness*, not only on account of the mildness of its
government, but the beauty and fertility of the
country), exhibit spots, that from the variety,
richness, and contrast of their parts, invite the
pencil of the Artist.—But in none of them can
thefe requisites more abound, than in the places
which are the subject of the following pages;

the

the Ifle of Wight and its vicinities being allowed to yield a rich affemblage of all thofe beauties that enchant the eye.

To a defcription of thofe beauties, as they muft prefent themfelves to the imagination of every one that has a tafte for picturefque fcenes, fhall we chiefly confine ourfelves; interfperfing only fuch hiftorical traits of the fituation, productions, antiquities, curiofities, &c. as may tend to relieve the fubject.

During the courfe of the Tour, the Author fometimes travelled alone, and fometimes in company; as will appear from his frequently ufing throughout the work, both the pronouns *I* and *we*.

It may be neceffary to obferve, that in the comparifons made with the works of the modern Artifts referred to, the fcenes or colouring which moft forcibly ftruck him, were the ftile, and the time of the day that each Artift courted.

And

And it might be no lefs needful to add, that as
he does not profefs to be deeply verfed in natural
hiftory and antiquity, he trufts his obfervations on
the natural productions and antiquities of the
Ifle of Wight, will not be too minutely criticifed
by fuch as are more ftudied in thofe fciences,
fhould he have been miftaken in any points. To
have paffed them entirely over, would have appeared neglectful ; he therefore has noticed them
as they fell in his way, defigning his remarks rather as hints for their fpeculation, or for their
amufement, than as exact and fcientific accounts.

The Picturefque Beauties of fuch particular
fcenes being conveyed by his eye to his mind,
were inftantly on the fpot noted by his pen ; and
the defcriptive remarks will, he flatters himfelf,
afford pleafure, not only to thofe who read his
work in the clofet, but alfo to thofe who may
have an opportunity of viewing the fame fcenes.

J. HASSELL.

ERRATA.

Page 27, line 17, for *Harry the Eighth also laid*, read *Henry the Sixth laid*.

Page 170, line 16, for *allum*, read *allum stones*.

Page 193 line, 12, for *is in for man*, read *is in form an*.

L I S T

OF

SUBSCRIBERS.

HIS Royal Highnefs the Prince of Wales
His Royal Highnefs the Duke of York
His Royal Highnefs the Duke of Gloucefter

A.

Mr. Alexander, jun.
——— Angelo, fen. Efq.
J. Petit Andrews, Efq.
Mifs Auftin, Seven Oaks
Alexander Adair, Efq. Flixton-hall, Suffolk
Mr. Anderfon, bookfeller, Holborn—three copies
Mrs. Andrews, Weftwell, Oxon

Right

B.

Right Hon. Lord Viscount Belgrave—large paper
Robert Barlow, Esq. Hanover-square
——— Bull, Esq. Isle of Wight
Mr. Badger, Portsmouth-point
Wilson Braddyll, Esq. Bruton-street
Mr. Brimyard, Southampton
Mrs. Barker, Newman-street
Rev. Mr. Burn
Sir Brook Boothby, Bart.
Philip Burton, Esq. Hatton-garden
Mr. Burch
William Beckford, Esq. Stratton-street—large paper
Mrs. T. Blackford, Devonshire-street
Cumberland Bentley, Esq. Sebton-park, Suffolk
Miss D. Browne
Mr. Board
Mrs. Bowater
Charles Brooke, Esq. Throgmorton-street
Mrs. Bonell, Hanover-square
Miss Barrington, Great James-street, Bedford-square
Edward Wilbraham Bootle, Esq.
Mr. William Brown, bookseller, Strand—three copies
Mr. J. Bew, bookseller, Paternoster-row—six copies
Mr. R. Baldwin, bookseller, ditto—twenty copies
Mr. R. Blamire, bookseller, Strand—six copies
Mr. T. Booker, bookseller, New Bond-street—six copies

C.

Lord Carbery, Hill-ftreet—large paper
Sir Henry Cofby
Right Hon. General Conway
Mifs Clarke, Hammerfmith
Price Clarke, Efq.
John Croft, Efq.
Mr. Coffer
Mr. Cheffon, New College, Oxford
Mr. James Coggant
Mr. Cleverley, Lifle-ftreet
Countefs of Coventry
R. Comyn, Efq. Inner Temple
James Cockerell, Efq. Brading, Ifle of Wight
Mr. Samuel Crane, Liverpool—fix copies
John Croft, Efq. jun.
Mr. William Clarke, bookfeller, New Bond-ftreet—fix
  copies

D.

—— Dafhwood, Efq.
J. Dornford, Efq. Lincoln's Inn
Lady Cottrell Dormer, Wimpole-ftreet
Her Grace the Duchefs of Devonfhire—large paper
Right Hon. Lord Duncannon
Right Hon. Lady Duncannon
Mrs. Denne, Bedford-row
Mrs. Dallafield
Rev. Rowland Duer, Chichefter, Suffex
W. Dowdefwell, Efq. Stratton-ftreet

Mr. Debrett,

Mr. Debrett, bookfeller, Piccadilly—twelve copies
Sir Henry Dafhwood, Bart.
Rev. Thomas Dalton, B. D. Vicar of Carifbrook
—— Dickens, Efq.
John Dennifon, Efq.—large paper
Mr. Charles Dilly, bookfeller, Poultry—ten copies

E.

Hon. G. Keith Elphinftone
Meffrs. Egertons, bookfellers, Charing-crofs—twelve copies
Lady Edmonftone, Argyle-ftreet
Meffrs. Elliot and Kay, bookfellers, Strand—fix copies
Mr. J. Evans, bookfeller, Paternofter-row—twenty-five copies
Mr. Edwards, bookfeller, Pall-mall—twenty-five copies
Mr. Earl, bookfeller, Frith-ftreet—three copies

F.

—— Forrefter, Efq. Temple—large paper
Mr. Richard Frewick
Mr. D. C. Fabian
Mr. Fearnfide
Captain Fruin, Southampton
G. Forbes, Efq. America-fquare
Mr. Jofeph Farmer
Mr. C. Forfter, bookfeller, Poultry—fix copies
Mr. Fry, Lincoln's Inn
Mr. John Forbes, bookfeller, Covent-garden—fix copies
Mr. Faulder, bookfeller, New Bond-ftreet—twenty-five copies

—— Gregory,

G.

—— Gregory, Efq.

Sir John Smythe Gardiner, Bart.

William Gee, Efq.

Mr. William Garret, Portfmouth

Mr. H. Gardiner, bookfeller, Strand—fourteen copies

Walwyn Graves, Efq.

Rev. James Gill, Cowes

Edmund Green, Efq. Medham, Ifle of Wight

Mr. J. Goodhew

William Gery, Efq. Bufhmead Priory, Bedfordfhire

G. Grote, Efq. Threadneedle-ftreet

H.

Mr. Charles Haley, Wigmore-ftreet

—— Hobbs, Efq. Bond-ftreet

Mr. J. Hall, bookfeller, Margate

Thomas Hibbert, Efq.

Mr. Hooper, bookfeller, Holborn

—— Hill, Efq. Gray's Inn

Mrs. Harlow, bookfeller, St. James's-ftreet—twelve copies

Francis Hanrot, Efq.

Right Hon. Lady Hawkefbury

Mr. John Hale, Bufh-lane

Hon. Mrs. Harcourt, Portland-place

J.

Mr. Jeffreys, bookfeller, Pall-mall—fix copies

Mrs. Joye, Sackville-ftreet

b 3

Mr. Edward

Mr. Edward Jenden, Swallow-street

Mr. Jeffrey, Throgmorton-street

Mr. William Jones, Dublin—two copies

Lady James

Mr. J. Johnson, bookseller, St. Paul's Church-yard—twelve copies

Mr. J. Jolliffe, bookseller, St. James's-street—six copies

K.

Mr. Henry Kinfit, Skinner's-hall, London

Mr. Robert Knight, Cheapside

L.

John Langstone, Esq. Clifford-street

Lady Loftus

Charles Lutwidge, Esq.

Mrs. Catharine Lockwood

Mr. L. Lee, New College, Oxford

Mrs. W. Larkins

Richard Lawrence, Esq.

Mr. Loton, King-street, Westminster

Peter Le Souif, Esq. No. 14, Broad-street-buildings

Thomas Lowes, Esq. Hartford-street

Miss Lewis, Queen-Ann-street

Mr. Thomas Lewis, bookseller, Covent-garden—six copies

Mr. B. Law, bookseller, Ave-Maria-lane—six copies

Mr. T. Longman, bookseller, Paternoster-row—six copies

John

M.

John Manners, jun. Efq. Pall-mall
Doctor John Munro
John Myrick, Efq.
Right Hon. Lady Mountftuart
—— Middleton, Efq. Upper Harley-ftreet
Mr. Thomas Miller, bookfeller, Bungay, Suffolk
Count of Maltzan, Hollies-ftreet, Cavendifh-fquare
Doctor John Moore, Clifford-ftreet
B. Mathews, Efq. Argyle-ftreet
Rev. Mr. J. Middleton
Mr. James Milne, Lower Grofvenor-ftreet
Mr. James Mathews, bookfeller, Strand—fix copies
Mr. J. Murray, bookfeller, Fleet-ftreet—twelve copies

N.

Hon. Mr. Naffau
David Nefbett, Efq. Marlborough-ftreet

O.

Mr. William Otridge, bookfeller, Strand—fix copies

P.

Sir Ralph Payne
George Porter, Efq.
Mr. J. Papineau, Carfhalton
John Purling, Efq. Portland-place
P. L. Powys, Efq. firft regiment of grenadier guards

Mr. John

Mr. John Preſtwidge

Lady Peaſhall

Henry James Pye, Eſq. Palace-yard

Mr. Poynter

Mr. Phillips, bookſeller, George-yard—ſix copies

Miſs Penn, Spring-gardens

Mr. John Paul

Samuel Prime, Eſq.

Mr. Thomas Payne, bookſeller, Mews-gate—ſix copies

Mr. Parſons, bookſeller, Paternoſter-row—three copies

R.

—— Robinſon, Eſq. Pall-mall

Meſſrs. Robinſons, bookſellers, Paternoſter-row —fifty
copies

Mr. Randal, Chelſea

Thomas Roberts, jun. Eſq.

Mr. Ray, Lincoln's Inn

Captain Reynolds, Prince of Wales's Military Academy,
Norland-houſe

Heneage Robinſon, clerk, A. M.

Mr. Robſon, bookſeller, New Bond-ſtreet—ſix copies

Mr. William Richardſon, bookſeller, Royal-Exchange—
twelve copies

Meſſrs. J. Rivington and Sons, bookſellers, St. Paul's
Church-yard—ſix copies

S.

Right Hon. Lady Charles Spencer

William Sharpe, Eſq.

F. Slipper, Eſq. Taviſtock-ſtreet, Bedford-ſquare

Hon.

Hon. Herbert Stuart

Robert Shuttleworth, Efq.

Thomas Sayer, Efq. Snachup, Herts

George Shipley, Efq. Horfeley Down

Right Hon. Lord Le De Spencer, Hanover-fquare

Mr. Styles, Tower Terrace

Mifs Eliza Slaney, No. 14, Norton-ftreet

Mifs Smart, Hampftead

Mr. Valentine Simmons, Margate

Mr. P. Sandford

—— Sales, Efq. Gower-ftreet

Thomas Sykes, Efq.

Mr. John Sewell, bookfeller, Cornhill—twelve copies

Thomas Salkeld, Efq.

Mr. Robert Stone, Bungay, Suffolk

Sir John Smith, Bart. Sydling, Dorfet

Mr. Shirley, Woolmer

Mr. Sanford

Mr. Thomas Smith, Bond-ftreet

Mr. John Stockdale, bookfeller, Piccadilly—fifty copies

Mr. S. Southern, bookfeller, St. James's-ftreet—fix copies

Mr. C. Stalker, bookfeller, Stationer's-court—fix copies

Meffrs. Scatcherd and Whitaker, bookfellers, Ave-Maria-lane—fix copies

Meffrs. Shepperfon and Reynolds, bookfellers, Oxford-ftreet—fix copies

Mr. Symonds, bookfeller, Paternofter row—twelve copies

T.

Mr. Terry, Clatterford, Ifle of Wight

—— Tunftall, Efq.

Sir John Trevelyan, Bart.

S. Tolfrey,

S. Tolfrey, Efq.

Sterne Tighe, Efq. Albemarle-ftreet—large paper

Jeremiah Tinker, Efq. Weybridge, Surrey.

Earl of Tankerville—large paper

U. V.

Earl of Uxbridge

Mr. T. Vernor, bookfeller, Birchin-lane—fix copies

W.

Earl of Wemyfs—large paper

Colonel Wemyfs

John Wilkes, Efq.

Mr. B. Wild, Newport

Mrs. Weft, Ryder-ftreet

John Wooll, Efq. Twyford

Mifs Weft

James Walley, Efq.

Mrs. Wild, Speen, Berks

Mrs. Whitaker, Kenfington—three copies

William Wilfon, Efq. Kenfington

William Wotton, Efq. Brook-ftreet

Hon. Mr. Walpole, Berkley-fquare

Mr. Thomas Wilkes

Mr. Thomas Wright

Bifhop of Winchefter

Alexander Wood, Efq. Golden-fquare

Mr. Walter, bookfeller, Piccadilly—fix copies

Mr. Walford, Clare Priory, Suffolk

Mr. Edmund White, Mile-end

James Walker, Efq.—large paper

Mr. Webfter,

Mr. Webfter, Fleet-ftreet

Major White

Mrs. Warden, Somerfet-ftreet

Mr. J. Walter, bookfeller, Charing-crofs.—fix copies

Meffrs. B. White and Son, bookfellers, Fleet-ftreet — fix copies

Meffrs. G. and T. Wilkie, bookfellers, St. Paul's Church-yard—fix copies

Y.

Mr. Young, engraver to the Prince of Wales

CONTENTS.

G. Owen, Efq. Norfolk-ftreet, Strand

Mr. William Anderfon, Gracechurch-ftreet

Thomas Morton, Efq. India-Houfe

George Hibbert, Efq.

Richard Trewin, Efq.

Mr. Powick

Sir John Thorold, Bart.—large paper

B. Grey, Efq. Lancafter

Richard Gough, Efq.

Mr. Edward Johnfon

Colonel Innes, Jofton-Houfe, High Wycombe, Bucks

Rev. James Ward, Queen's College, Cambridge

William Miller, Efq. Cheltenham

CONTENTS OF THE FIRST VOLUME.

SECTION VII.

SECTION VIII.

SECTION IX.

SECTION

SECTION X.

SECTION XI.

SECTION XII.

SECTION XIII.

TOUR

TOUR

OF

THE ISLE OF WIGHT.

SECTION I.

HAVING left London during the laſt ſummer, in order to make our intended Tour of the Iſle of Wight, we paſſed through Hammerſmith and Hounſlow, to Egham; near which lies the famous mead wherein king John executed the charter which proved the foundation of our preſent happy conſtitution. From Egham, we proceeded through a part of Windſor Foreſt, ſo beautifully deſcribed by Pope, to Bagſhot Heath.

Adjacent to the heath, on the right hand, stands a villa, where we could not help remarking a cascade, in which one of those beauties seems to be aimed at, where *Art* can never possibly rival *Nature*. It consists of a combined small parcel of stones, regularly placed, over which is conducted a small stream, that, by the time it has passed the first row of stones, appears like several water-pipes playing down a smooth passage, and disgusts the picturesque eye.

Leaving Bagshot, we traversed the heath on the left; Blackwater &c. lying on the right. Surely, even to view this heath, is a sufficient temptation for the many depredations that are committed on it. The length of it is so dreary, and the gloom which overspreads it so horrid, that even the lively month of June can scarcely erase the marks of terror that incessantly present themselves to the traveller's eye. From Egham, till you arrive within three or four miles of Farnham, a tract of near twenty miles, the country round exhibits a most desolate scene.

Farnham

Farnham is scarcely seen till you are close upon it. This town lies in a pleasant valley, and is well watered. The ouzy soil, by which it is entirely surrounded, is appropriated to the growth of hops, and usually stands the farmers in from ten to twenty-two pounds per acre. The hops produced here are acknowledged to be the best in England.

The bishop of Winchester's palace is situated on a rising ground. It was built by king Stephen, for the use of his brother, Henry de Blois, bishop of Winchester, and continued for some time to belong to the royal family; but in a subsequent reign it was affixed to the see of Winchester, and is now the chief summer residence of the present bishop. The numerous possessors of this ancient building have almost metamorphosed it. The castle still remains; and the top of it is nearly an acre of ground, converted into a fruit garden. At the bottom of the castle are the remains of a thick wall, which formerly served as a redoubt; below that, what was then a deep ditch, is now a kitchen garden.

From

From the top of the caftle are feen very extenfive views. Suffex appears quite clofe; while the utmoft limits of Hampfhire fcarcely bound the horizon. Berkfhire, to the north-weft, binds its other diftance; and the delightful fpot belonging to Mr. Bacon, called Moore Park, affords another agreeable view.

In the laft mentioned retired fpot, dean Swift wrote many of his works; the proprietor of it at that time, being his moft particular friend. That celebrated author, and his hoft, paffed the principal part of their leifure hours on Crookfbury Hill, and at night, having reviewed the compofitions of the day, committed fuch parts as on a revifal did not pleafe, to the flames.

From Farnham to Alton is an agreeable and picturefque country.—A noble range of woods, the property of lord Stawell, form a variety of fide-fcreens for a picture. But the views, in general, though pleafing, are very contracted.—A fufficient quantity of water meanders through the valley from

Farnham

Farnham, which adds frequent beauties to the fcenes. The old Roman road that led from Winchefter, their *Vente Belgarium*, to London, is ftill difcernable as far as Alton.

A continued famenefs reigns all the way from Alton to Alresford. At the entrance of this town are feen the feats of colonels Rodney and Sheriffe. That which is built of brick, is the property of the former; the white one, of the latter. The duke of Chandos has a feat about five miles from Alresford, called Alvingdon; but nothing of antiquity lies near it.

About a mile from Alresford, a moft delightful valley prefents itfelf;—well wooded and watered;—while here and there a ftraggling cottage, burfting from a clump of trees, enlivens the rural fcenes.

We now enter the downs of Winchefter; —a profpect entirely different from what we had hitherto feen. On the firft afcent, the woody parts towards Southampton fkirt the horizon; while a turnpike in the

B 3   middle

middle of a fmall copfe breaks the firft diftance;—each hill gradually rifing over another, and terminating in a foft confufion.

Winchefter is fituated in a valley, through
which the river Itching takes its courfe,
and is navigable up to the eaft end of the
town, where there is a wharf; at which the
barges from Southampton and the adjacent
country, unload.

We find this city to have been no inconfiderable place, fo far back as the reign
of king Athelftone; who granted it the
privilege of fix mints for the coinage of
money. It was frequently the refidence of
the Weft Saxon kings, who held their courts
here; and one of whom erected it into a
bifhop's fee, by tranflating the bifhopric of
Dorchefter hither. It has been three times
burnt down; and about the year 860 was
demolifhed by the Danes.

Clofe by the weft gate ftands king Arthur's palace. Egbert, the firft Saxon king
in whom the fovereignty of all England
was

was vefted, was crowned in it; and after
him Alfred, and Edward the Confeffor; befides feveral other princes of the Saxon line.
The unfortunate Rufus made a point of being crowned here every Chriftmas; and
Richard Cœur de Lion, after his arrival
from the holy wars, and the long impri-
fonment he had undergone during his return, was a fecond time crowned in this
caftle. Henry the Fifth held his parliament
here, before he embarked for France.

In the reign of Stephen, we find it again
defolated. The emprefs Maud, during the
civil wars of that period, having gained a
complete victory over the forces of the king,
fhe fixed her head quarters in this city; but
the inhabitants not being well affected to
her caufe, with the affiftance of Henry de
Blois, the king's brother, at that time bifhop
of the diocefe, they betrayed it into the
hands of Stephen, and Maud narrowly
efcaped being made prifoner. This fhe ef-
fected by ftratagem; caufing herfelf to be
conveyed out of the town as a corpfe,
through the thickeft of her enemies.

B 4
During

During Cromwell's wars, it was feveral times befieged by the parliament's forces, and at laft was taken by fir William Waller, one of their generals, who again demolifhed the greateft part of it.

In the county hall we fee the famous round table of king Arthur. It is compofed of a folid piece of wood, eighteen feet in diameter. The people of the town trace its antiquity to the time of king Arthur, twelve hundred years back, while others fuppofe its origin to be of a much more modern date. Tournaments were held here by Arthur's knights, before the king and his court.

Adjoining to the chapel, and on the fpot where the caftle once ftood, fir Chriftopher Wren, by command of king Charles the Second, formed a defign for a palace, in which that monarch intended to entertain his whole court, and to amufe them with various kinds of divertizements. And though this plan was only in part carried into execution, the building is magnificent and

and fpacious, the fouth fide being two hundred and fixteen feet long, the weft three hundred and twenty-eight feet; and notwithftanding it is but a fhell, it coft upwards of twenty-five thoufand pounds. The grand duke of Tufcany prefented Charles with feveral marble pillars of exquifite workmanfhip, which were to have fupported the roof of the grand ftair-cafe. Thefe were afterwards given by George the Firft to the duke of Bolton. A handfome balluftrade runs quite round the top, and the infide of the court is adorned with porticos. Had the whole of the plan been executed, it would have been a palace worthy of the gay and expenfive monarch who caufed it to be erected; but his death happening before it was completed, the further profecution of it was laid afide; and the only ufe it has been put to fince, is being made a place of confinement for the French and Spanifh prifoners taken during our late wars.

In a meadow adjacent to the town, called Danemarck Mead, the famous Guy earl of Warwick is faid to have encountered and vanquifhed Colbrand, the Danifh giant.

The

The prefent cathedral, which is a grand and venerable ftructure, was founded about the year 1070, by bifhop Walkelyn, a Norman, under the patronage of William the Conqueror, and dedicated to St. Swithin. After this, William of Wykeham improved it ; but bifhop Fox is faid to have brought it to its prefent ftate.

After nine hundred years endowment, it was feized, with the reft of the church lands, by Henry the Eighth, and the plate, ornaments, and images, converted to his ufe, and depofited in his treafury. Having given this proof of his love for the church, he re-eftablifhed it on its prefent foundation, and as fome recompence for his depredations, granted permiffion to dedicate it to the Holy Trinity. Since that period, it is frequently called Trinity Church. The clerical eftablifhment confifts of one dean, twelve prebendaries, fix minor canons, ten lay-clerks, and eight chorifters, befides feveral other members.

The length of the cathedral from eaft to
weft

weſt is 545 feet, including the chapel, which is 54 feet. The choir is 136 feet long. From the iron door to the porch at the weſt end is 351 feet; the tranſceps 186; the part below them 87 feet; and the choir 40. The tower is 138 feet high, its width 50 feet by 48, and it is about 25 feet and an half above the roof.

The building is of Gothic architecture, and truly ſublime in its appearance. It is generally allowed to be nearly equal to that of the abbey church at St. Alban's. In two receſſes, as you approach the choir, are the ſtatues of James and Charles, the Firſt. They are both of copper, but were horridly defaced during the civil wars which took place in the reign of the latter.

In the pannels under the organ are ſome memorials relative to Henry the Eighth's foundation, dated 1540;—the arms of the firſt dean, William Kingſmill;—the garter and mitre of the biſhops of Wincheſter;— with the letter S, and another initial letter, the greateſt part of which is obliterated.

Under

Under a plain monument, without any inscription, lies William Rufus; the manner of whose death is too well known to need repeating here. During the civil wars in the reign of Charles the First, the rebels paid this son of the Conqueror a visit, and as a proof of their dislike to monarchy, stripped his remains of a robe of gold cloth, a ring set with rubies, and a few other matters that were interred with him.

This cathedral, I believe, has to boast the remains of as many kings as any other in England; for we find that the chief part, both of the Saxon and the Norman line, rest under its roof. Bishop Fox spared no pains to collect the bones of these kings, and of every other person of distinction, and carefully deposited them in six gilded coffins, or chests, superbly carved, which he caused to be placed on a wall on the south side of the choir. These chests bore the date of 1525.

Statues of solid silver formerly stood in niches, where now stand mouldering urns.

They

They were the gift of bifhop Harris, who likewife prefented the church with the marble pavement that leads to the high altar. The ftained glafs is alfo his gift ; with two pinnacles, and fome other ornamental architecture with which he fronted the outfide boundary of the choir, in the midft of which ftands his own ftatue epifcopally habited.

Cromwell's army, ever intent on plunder, and ever ready to teftify their hatred to the church, entered this cathedral on the 16th of December 1642, and committed the moft horrid outrages. Among other acts of wanton facrilege, they deftroyed the beautiful carved work in the choir, broke the organ to pieces, feized on all the valuables, overturned the communion table, and burnt the rails that encompaffed it. Nor did their rapacious hands ftop here ; but getting at the chefts of bones which bifhop Fox had collected, they threw them againft the windows of ftained glafs, jocularly obferving as they did it, that it was the refurrection of the dry bones. And to thefe ravages was
Waller

Waller a witnefs, without endeavouring to put a ftop to them. They likewife defaced many beautiful pieces of antiquity, and taking away the croffes, popifh books, and pictures, made a fham proceffion with them; after which they committed them to the flames.

The weft window, with a few others, fortunately efcaped their depredations; as likewife did the magnificent tomb of William of Wykeham, which was happily prevented from fharing the fame fate by the refolution and perfeverance of one Cuff, an officer in Waller's army, who had formerly been a ftudent of the college.

Over the communion-table is a picture painted by Mr. Weft. The gentlemen who fixed it up, finding it larger than the place appropriated for it, cut off two of the principal figures in the fore ground, which has confiderably defaced the piece. The fubject of it is the raifing of Lazarus;—a moft charming picture;—the colouring not inferior to Titian's;—the drawings wonderfully

fully correct;—the hand of death feems indeed to have laid faft hold on Lazarus; while the fpirit and animation of the other figures add double force to the part with which they are contrafted.

In the chapel of the Virgin Mary, ftands the monument of the earl of Portland, who was lord high treafurer in the reign of Charles the Firft. His effigy is at full length, raifed on three pillars, and accoutred in copper armour.

There is another chapel on the fouth, called Silkeftede. It is doubtful whether this perfon is the founder of the chapel; but certain it is that he altered fome parts of it, from an infcription of T S near the library window.

At the eaft end of the fouth wall are depofited the remains of bifhop Fox. His monument is a capital fpecimen of Gothic architecture.—There is no infcription on it.—A fkeleton is the only emblem affixed to the tomb.

Here

Here also rests cardinal Beaufort, who was a liberal benefactor to the cathedral. The emblematical figure reclining on his tomb, is arrayed in a cardinal's habit. The mutilated effigy attending, is supposed to be St. Swithin; it was partly of brass; but, as in many other instances, so little respect did Cromwell's soldiers pay either to saint or apostle, that you barely trace any remains of what appears to have been once a beautiful figure.

The following curious inscription is on a monument the south side of the choir. The person who promises so acceptable a reward to every good catholic praying for his soul, was prior of the convent. It runs thus—

Hic jacit GULIELMUS DE BASING, quondam prior istius ecclesiæ, cujus animæ propitietur Deus; et qui pro anima ejus oraverit, tres annos et quinquaginta dies indulgentia precipit.

In English thus;

Here lies William of Basing, formerly prior of this church, to whose soul may God be propitious; and he who shall pray for him, shall obtain an indulgence of three years and fifty days.

Many

Many other curious tombs and monu-
ments are to be feen in this cathedral, but
the foregoing will ferve as a fufficient fpecimen.

On the fouth fide of the cathedral ftands
Winchefter college, founded by William of
Wykeham, who was liberal in his benefac-
tions to it, as well as to New College, Oxford. The foundation was laid by him on
the 26th day of March 1387. It originally
confifted of a warden and feventy fcholars,
ten priefts, three chaplains, three clerks,
and fixteen chorifters, with one fchool-maf-
ter, and an ufher.

In this college is an emblematical paint-
ing, reprefenting a trufty fervant. The de-
vice confifts of the figure of an afs, with
human hands, and ftag's feet ;—a padlock
faftened to his fnout ;—a fhield hanging on
his arm, with a fword by his fide; and
he bears in his left hand implements of
induftry. This emblematical figure is intended to denote patience, fwiftnefs, cou-
rage, fecrecy, and labour ; the needful cha-

Vol. I.   C   racteriftics

racteriftics of a good fervant. Taken altogether, it is at beft but a whimfical jum-
ble of the artift.

A room, weft of the cloifters, in the
college, contains the rules and orders of
every clafs belonging to it. They are infcribed on the walls.

In the high ftreet of Winchefter is the
market crofs, forty three feet in height.
Some will have it that this edifice was
erected at a very early period, in comme-
moration of the introduction of chriftianity:
while others fuppofe it to have been founded fo late as the reign of Henry the Sixth.
At all events it remains a perfect mark of
the fuperftition of the times.

It is a moft elegant pile of Gothic building. In one of the niches ftands the figure of St. John in the act of preaching;
but fo wretchedly has it been bedaubed
by the painter, that the chief beauties of
the fculpture is hidden. The wife men of
Winchefter, fome years back, had determi-
ned

ned to pull this noble ſtructure down ; and had not ſome ſpirited gentlemen of the county ſtrongly oppoſed the deſign, it would have undergone a Cromwellian operation. It thus eſcaped their unhallowed hands ;—but ſo terribly disfigured is it by their beautifying, (as they term it) that, except the general appearance of the architecture, little elſe is to be ſeen worth notice, all the inſcriptions being obliterated.

The hoſpital and church of Saint Croſs, are well worthy the traveller's notice. They are in the Saxon ſtile, and were built during the reign of king Stephen. By the inſtitution of the founder, every traveller who knocks at the door of this hoſpital in his way, may claim a manchet of white bread and a cup of beer ; a good quantity of which is daily ſet apart to be given away.

Time hurrying us, and a gloomy evening impelling us to haſten our journey, we took our leave of Wincheſter without making any further obſervations. A violent ſtorm of rain, thunder and lightning, however,

overtaking

overtaking us, foon after we had left the city, and obliging us to feek for fhelter, we once more returned to it; and having again perambulated the town, we left it the next morning without regret. For a place of fuch confequence, we were not a little fur-prized at its mean appearance; the ftreets are narrow and inconvenient, and the houfes in general low and inelegant. The water of Alresford paffes through the heart of the city, and joins its ftream to Itching river.

Though there is neither much trade, nor any manufactory worthy of notice carried on at Winchefter, the pleafantnefs of its fi-tuation, from the extenfive plains and downs by which it is furrounded, makes its envi-rons the refidence of many perfons of for-tune and refpectability.

Scarcely any thing new is feen till you reach Hurfley, a beautiful little village, five miles beyond Winchefter. On the right hand of it ftands the feat of fir William Heathcote, furrounded by the moft luxuri-ant verdure that Hampfhire can boaft. The

venerable

venerable oak and ſtately pine, vying with each other in grandeur, entirely overſhadow the village.—This range of woods takes a long ſweep from Romſey towards Botley.

About a mile beyond Hurſley we enter-ed Southampton Common, and for the firſt time had a view of the ſea. Unfortunately for us, the weather was hazy, and we had but an indifferent proſpect either of that, or of the ſurrounding country.

On the moſt elevated part of the farther ſide of the common, is the ſummer houſe of Mr. Fleming ;—an elegant little build-ing, commanding an extenſive view of the adjacent hills, and likewiſe of the Iſle of Wight, which from this deſirable ſpot, in a clear day, has every beauty that a pleaſing combination of wood and water can give it. Several gentlemens' ſeats ſkirt the road ſide, ſo that it appears one continued ſcene of lively vegetation.

C 3 SECTION

SECTION II.

WE had now reached Hampton, or, as it is at prefent called, Southampton, which lies twelve miles from Winchefter, and about twenty-fix from Portfmouth; its fituation being high, and the fea coming up to the quay, renders it a delightful fummer refidence.

We can trace back the origin of this town to the year 47, when it was invaded by the Romans; who were frequently defeated and driven back by the Britons refident in and about the foutheromoft coaft of England. This people, however, afterwards eftablifhed a colony here, or rather at the old town, which ftood more to the eaftward, to which they gave the name of Claufentum.

In the year 512, Cerdic, king of the Weft Saxons, made a fuccefsful attempt upon Hantun, as it was then called. Here he defeated the Britifh king Aurelius Ambrofius, who having gained a very confiderable

derable victory over Hengift, was fo elated
by his fuccefs, that laying afide the pru-
dence for which he had hitherto been
famed, he fuffered himfelf to be out-gene-
raled and vanquifhed by Cerdic. The famous king Arthur was likewife flain by this
Saxon about twenty years after.

It was here that Canute the Great re-
proved his courtiers for their flattery, when
they affured him that even the waves of the
fea would obey him.

About the year 1020, this town was entirely demolifhed by the Danes; who,
wherever they came, diftinguifhed themfelves by their rapacious and barbarous
deeds. The moft unheard-of cruelties were
ufually committed by them whenever they
happened to be victorious.

While the victorious Edward the Third
was in France, afferting his right to the
throne of that kingdom, the fon of the
king of Sicily was difpatched, on their
part, to make depredations on the coaft

C 4 of

of England. This commiffion proved fatal to Southampton; for the French landing there, reduced it to afhes. They were however foon after repulfed by the Englifh, who, collecting together an army from the troops in the Weftern parts, marched againft the invaders, and having entirely defeated them, obliged them to re-imbark with the lofs of their commander.

Here it was that king Henry the Fifth embarked when he fet out upon his expedition againft that kingdom. Previous to his failing, the French having remitted a large fum of money to Cambridge, Scroop, and Gray, the favourites of the king, they entered into a confpiracy againft him; but their treacherous defigns were happily put a ftop to by the earl of March. That nobleman, who had been inadvertently drawn into the plot, forefeeing the fatal confequences it muft be productive of to his royal mafter, to whom he was bound not only by the ties of allegiance, but of gratitude, divulged the fecret, and thereby fruftrated their plans. The earl of Cambridge

and

and Sir Thomas Gray were beheaded; while lord Scroop, rendered doubly blameable by his ingratitude, the king having conferred upon him great honours, and repofed in his bofom his choiceft fecrets, was hanged, drawn, and quartered.

The merchants of the port of Southampton were, during fome centuries, the greateft importers of wine in the kingdom, excepting thofe of London. The privileges relative to this article of commerce, granted them in their charter by king Henry the Second, and afterwards confirmed and renewed by king John, were fo extenfive and confiderable, that the merchants of Briftol, and thofe of the other ports on the weft and fouth coafts of England, were obliged to land their wines here, and after having paid the duties, then to re-fhip, and carry them to their own ports.

The difpofal of a part of thefe privileges, fome years ago, to the city of Briftol, has fixed an indelible ftigma on the corporation. Nor are the corporation of the prefent day undeferving

undeferving of cenfure, for fuffering the river near the quay to remain in its prefent
ftate. The mud is fo deep, at and near the
landing place, that at low water a boat can
neither take you off, nor bring you afhore;
to the very great inconvenience in particular of the paffengers going to or coming
from, the Ifle of Wight. It is no uncommon thing to fee a great number of paffengers in the Cowes packet, which had happened to lofe the tide, wait fome hours on
board for the return of it; many of whom
when it has rained, from the fmallnefs of
the cabin, and the confequent want of fhelter, have been thoroughly wet. And even
the fteps leading to the landing place are in
a wretched condition. The fmall quay is,
if poffible, many degrees worfe than the
other; fo that a boat, even at high water, is
there difagreeably circumftanced.

Southampton was once walled round; and
many parts of the walls are ftill ftanding.
They are compofed of very large ftones,
full of fmall white fhells, and have many
lunettes and towers. In fome places it is
furrounded

furrounded with a double ditch. There were formerly four gates to it; but only three of them are now ftanding. The firft is at the entrance of the town, and is generally termed Bar Gate; the fecond was called the Eaft Gate, but of this not a veftige now remains; the third is South Gate, which is made a place of confinement for debtors; and the fourth is Water Gate, at the bottom of which is the contemptible little quay before fpoken of.

Oliver Cromwell's ruffians were likewife bufied here upon fome excellent carved work and ftained glafs, belonging to Bugle Hall in this town, which was deftroyed by thefe lawlefs depredators.

Harry the Eighth alfo laid his facred hands on the manufactory of allum foil carried on here, in which the merchants had property to the amount of near ten thoufand pounds; but in order to counterbalance his depredations by fome favor, as his ufual cuftom was, he permitted them for a certain time to land goods free of duty. He

failed

failed not, however, to feize on the valuable trade for tin, that was alfo carried on here.

Charles the Firft confirmed the charter that had been granted by Henry the Second, and inftituted a corporation; which confifts of a mayor, a recorder, a fheriff, and two bailiffs: all thofe who have ferved any of the foregoing offices, conftitute the common council; and they who have paffed the chair, are aldermen. An unlimited number of burgeffes may likewife be elected at the will of the mayor and council.

The falubrious air of Southampton is a fufficient inducement for the great refort of valetudinarians, and others, there is to it. Nor are the general accommodations lefs refpectable than the town is inviting. Several country feats round it render the walks at once agreeable and pleafant. But after having trod every rural walk and pleafant path that Southampton has to boaft, Netley Abbey, of which two views are annexed, will be found to enjoy the preeminence.

Having

—Having paffed Itching ferry in our way to the abbey, we crofs the grounds of N. Dance, Efq. R. A. at Woolfon, whofe feat commands at every curve, a frefh view of the beauties of Hampton river; an exten- five thicket catches the roving eye. On the foot road to the abbey, the diftance is like- wife pleafantly diverfified.

In a fmall dell, by the fide of a wood, ftands this antique building;—and near it is the fort, which fronts the river.—A plea- fure known only to the contemplative mind, imperceptibly fteals into the breaft, on tak- ing a view of fo romantic and retired a place as Netley Abbey. To a heart not in- fenfible to the calm enjoyments of fuch a retreat, the awfulnefs of the venerable pile, down whofe fide the lurking ivy fportively plays, together with the grandeur of the architecture, afford a fatisfaction, that the moft pleafurable fcenes of the gay circle cannot excite.—A thoufand agreeable ideas rufh into the mind, and we are loft in wonder and contemplation. By fuch a fcene as this, the youthful imagination is expand- ed

ed, and the genius directed to some useful
pursuit.—It sometimes leads to the study of
history ;—sometimes its softness and harmony aid the powers of music ;—and it
needs not be added, that it furnishes the artist with a delightful subject for his pencil.

Time has just brought this venerable pile,
as a piece of ruins, to its highest perfection.
A small but pleasing group of trees encircle it ;—while a bed of overgrown nettles,
rising stately at every avenue, form an
agreeable relief to its mouldering sides.

It is the property of Mr. Dance ; and
much to that gentleman's credit, he endeavours to preserve this piece of antiquity from demolition. A married servant
of his resides about a quarter of a mile from
the spot, where refreshments may be procu-
red. Frequent aquatic excursions are made
from Hampton to drink tea in the abbey,
and every accommodation for that purpose
is furnished by the civil and industrious pair
who are appointed to take care of it.

Various

Various are the opinions relative to the founder of this abbey; fome attributing it to Peter de Rupibus; others to Henry III. But it is generally believed that Henry built it. Certain it is that about the year 1239, he inftituted near this fpot a convent of monks, of the Ciftercian order, which he removed from the vicinity of Beaulieu. Other endowments were beftowed upon it by John de Warenna, earl of Surry, in the year 1242. At the diffolution, it had an abbot and twelve monks, whofe revenues were valued at 100l. 12s. 8d. a year.

Such a place as this, that has been devoted to the purpofes of fuperftition, feldom fails to give birth to fuperftitious ftories. Among thofe told us, we fhall infert the two following; and as they are fomewhat fingular, and may furnifh a fubject of laughter to the incredulous, hope we fhall ftand excufed for the infertion.

Sir Bartlet Lucy, who was then the pof-feffor of the abbey, fold it to a taylor of Southampton; who bought it with a view
of

of making a profit of the materials. The taylor, or, as his defcendants, who are at this time refident in that place, fay, his wife, was informed in a dream, feveral nights fucceffively, that the moment he attempted to diflodge a fingle ftone, the whole fabric would fall upon him. And fo, as the account goes, it really happened. For difdaining to profit by any advice that came in fo queftionable a fhape, he began to pull it down; when, marvellous to relate, no fooner had he begun his unhallowed delapidations, than the large window and part of the ceiling fell on his head and fractured his fcull. We are further informed, that before he made his exit, he acknowledged to thofe around him that he had been warned by feveral apparitions, of the fatal confequences that would attend the facrilegious deed; and fell a facrifice to his incredulity.

Nor is a circumftance of a more recent date, which the perfon who fhows the abbey relates, lefs believed in the neighbourhood. A labouring man had for feveral nights dreamt that a cheft of money lay

buried

buried in the ruins. And fixing upon a
fpot near the entrance, began there to dig;
from whence, agreeable to the tenor of his
dream, he dug a cheft of ancient coins, of a
confiderable value. The mafter of the man
hearing of the affair, infifted upon their
being delivered up to him; and the unfortunate dreamer, in order to avoid a lawfuit
with which he was threatened, found himfelf obliged to refund the prognofticated
boon. The keeper ftill fhows you a heap
of ftones, which are faid to have inclofed
the cheft; and an old man, upwards of
eighty years of age, corroborated the truth
of the ftory, by vouching to us, that he had
himfelf feen the cheft, and that the metal
contained in it was really gold.

The entrance of the abbey, or what is
termed the fountain court, is a fquare, encircled with lofty walls. The kitchen is fuppofed to have led to fome fubterraneous
paffage.—On the right hand, at the further
corner, is the grand hall leading to the chapel, whofe venerable fides ftill boaft a flight
of fteps which range round part of the

building. The area at the bottom of the chapel is in a very rugged ftate, it being overgrown with nettles, which cover the fallen fragments of the roof, and not only incommode the paffenger, but are far from being pleafing to the eye.

The grandeur and elegance of the internal appearance of the abbey, is fuperior to any of the outfide views. The chapel, built in the fhape of a crofs, with feveral receffes communicating with the abbey,—and continued groups of lofty trees,—delightfully harmonize and variegate the infide. Grand and ftriking as the appearance of thefe ancient ruins are, they have undoubtedly received additional beauties from the elegant pen of Mr. Keate. Every part of it is fo truly, juftly, and picturefquely pourtrayed by him, that his Netley Abbey even vies with the original. How finely is the prefent delapidated ftate of it defcribed by him in the following ftanzas :

I hail

I hail at laſt theſe ſhades, this well-known wood,
 That ſkirts with verdant ſlope the barren ſtrand,
Where Netley's ruins, bordering on the flood,
 Forlorn in melancholy greatneſs ſtand.

How chang'd alas! from that rever'd abode
 Grac'd by proud majeſty in ancient days,
When monks recluſe theſe ſacred pavements trod,
 And taught th' unletter'd world its Maker's praiſe,

Now ſunk, deſerted, and with weeds o'ergrown,
 Yon proſtrate walls their harder fate bewail;
Low on the ground their topmoſt ſpires are thrown,
 Once friendly marks to guide the wand'ring ſail.

The ivy now, with rude luxuriance bends
 Its 'tangled foliage through the cloiſter'd ſpace,
O'er the green window's mould'ring height aſcends,
 And fondly claſps it with a laſt embrace.

Yon parted roof that nods aloft in air,
 The threat'ning battlement, the rifted tow'r,
The choir's looſe fragments ſcatter'd round, declare,
 Inſulting TIME, the triumphs of thy pow'r!

On the banks of the river ſtand the ruins of a caſtle that ſerved as a front to the abbey. It commands a very extenſive part of the river; but nothing now remains, except the walls, to remind us of the ſtrength it once poſſeſſed.

The

The ride to this fweet fpot is nearly ten miles, through a lovely fcene of wood and water. By the foot way it is three miles and an half from Southampton, acrofs the river Itching, where a ferry-boat conftantly plies. The walk to it is beautiful; nor is your return from it lefs fo. The town of Hampton, and its fpire, has a pleafing effect;—the New Foreft is in the diftance; but the view, in general, is too ftraggling and extenfive; the objects are not fufficiently combined for a picture, though pleafing to the eye.

Our next excurfion was to the priory of St. Denis, formerly the refidence of a brotherhood of black canons. It is fituated on the flowery banks of the river Itching, about three miles from its entrance, and exhibits a pile of antique ruins that are haftening to decay. Scarcely any part of the chapel is ftanding; and if the remains of the houfe are not fhortly fecured from the depredations of its inhabitants, and from the inceffant ravages of a great number of hogs, both that and the chapel will foon fhare the fate of many an ancient fabric, and leave no trace of its exiftence.

We

We have fcarcely any authentic intelligence from which to afcertain the founder of this priory. The leafe of the venerable pile is granted to the prefent poffeffor by general Stibbert, to whom we recommend the prefervation of its relics from entire obliteration, that it may ftill remain as an hiftorical record of ancient times, and contribute to the pleafure of every curious traveller who vifits Southampton.

It ftands near four miles from that town, and was viewed by us on one of thofe clear evenings, when the declining fun juft catching on the higheft fummit of the building, gave an agreeable relief to the fore ground, which, of courfe, lay in the fhadow; while his dazzling rays overtopped the neighbouring river, and added every luftre to the oppofite woody craggs, overhanging the fandy fhore, that the moft picturefque eye could wifh or defire.

In the road to this fmall but pleafant fpot, is the feat of general Stibbert. It is an elegant building, and commands very ex-

tenfive

tenfive views of the oppofite fhore ;—the New Foreft ;—Southampton River ;—Calfhot Caftle ;—and the Ifle of Wight. Several boxes belonging to other gentlemen fkirt the road, but none of them fo pleafant as this plain and neat fpot.

The feat of Mr. Sloane lies about two miles beyond general Stibbert's, in the middle of a little valley, that alfo commands the navigation of the river Itching. From this road you may proceed the carriage way to Netley Abbey, and to govenor Hornby's houfe.

On our left hand at the top of the hill, near the three mile ftone, on the road to London, is the fummer houfe of Mr Fleming, the member for Southampton.—We noticed this fpot on paffing Southampton Common ; but the fullen clouds lowering upon us at that time, we could only make tranfient remarks on it ;—but now viewed with a more compofed eye, a charming fcene difplays itfelf ;—a luxuriant hanging wood, forming the park, exhibits every

feature

feature of variegation that fuch a fcene can poffibly produce; over which a gentle de- fcent terminates into a foft furface of a fum- mer fea;—while many a proud veffel, im- patient for the wafting gale, difplays the livelieft reflections of the fhivering fail in the tranfparent ocean.

Far beyond thefe luxurious fcenes, a kind- lier fhore blends foftly in, and prefents its fpreading oaks, joined with the prouder fo- reft plants.

We fcarcely ever remember to have feen fo well chofen a fpot, from the choice of any gentleman, as this of Mr. Fleming's fummer houfe. We fometimes obferve that perfons of fortune, in chufing a fpot for erecting a feat, fix on fome obfcure place, where toil- fome labour endeavours, but in vain, to rival the vivid blooms that fair impatient Nature rears. A reclufe feat appears *fans* beauty, that the rifing hill demands; and at beft never difplays more than grovelling hufbandry.— How fuperior fuch commanding profpects as that under confideration ! and how mean

and

and contemptible, when compared with it, are the nicely trimmed yews that adorn the feat of the citizen!

The fummer rides about Southampton are fuch as few places can boaft.—An inconvenience attends the tide's retiring fo far, as you ride along the river's fide; neverthelefs the foft breezes that fan you while you traverfe its fhore, in fome meafure compenfate for this.

Southampton having been fixed on as the centre of our tour, our excurfions from it will be inferted as they take place, and the town and its environs defcribed occafionally, fo as to give a variety to our defcriptions.

As one part of our plan was to vifit parts of the New Foreft, we began our route from Southampton to Lymington, the neareft boundary of it towards the Ifle of Wight. The firft village we paffed after leaving the townw as Millbrook, which lies within about two miles from it ;—a pleafant

little

little ſpot, but we found nothing in it to engage the attention. From thence we croſſed Redbridge, and through Totten, reached the foreſt

Its entrance is not ſo ſtriking here, as it is in many other parts.—When you gain the firſt ſummit, a woody promontory ſkirts the road on the right ;—on the left, for three miles, a more open ſpace attracts the eye, terminated—as moſt of the diſtances in this part are—by a group of venerable oaks or lofty elms.

In the midſt of a plantation of oaks, reſides one of the keepers of the foreſt. His lodge, which is generally called by the country people Ironſhill, ſtands about a mile from the road, in one of thoſe grand receſſes where Nature ſtrews her favours with unbounded liberality.

When we view a pleaſing ſcene, that, in ſuch a country as Hampſhire, where every view is a picture, muſt frequently burſt upon the ſight, we at once feel its full force, but

but to what a pitch is the imagination carried, when we behold Nature flyly fporting,
in fome retired corner, where, as if fearful of being feen, fhe rears a ponderous
grove to overhang fome murmuring rivulet, to whofe chryftal ftream (fweet facred
haunt!) the timorous fawns or fturdy heifers retire to fhun the fcorching rays of
Phœbus. While fome ftand cheft high in
the rapid current to avoid their annoying
enemy the fly, others recline on the mofly
bank, and catch the paffing breeze. But if
perchance the ruder breath of Zephyr ruf-
tles through the leaves on the furrounding
boughs, away fly the fearful fawns, and,
bounding over the flowery lawn, feek a fe-
curer retreat.

From this romantic fcene we turned our
horfes to the left, and ftruck into the road
to Lindhurft, through a continued fhade of
overhanging wood. The evening being
clear, we were tempted to turn out of the
way to know from what caufe a ftrange
noife, which feemed to iffue from the brow
of an adjacent hill, originated. Upon reach-
ing

ing the fpot, we found it to be one of the forefters broufing the deer; and we were not a little pleafed at feeing fome hundreds of thefe wild inhabitants of the foreft bound-ing towards him, whenever they heard his well-known voice, and following him to the frefheft pafture, or to fhare in the fodder which he cut from the tender branches of the trees. Should any of the herd have ftrayed, he calls the wanderer back in a note not unlike the war-hoop of the Indian tribes.

The farmers who live in the vicinity of this part of the foreft ,are often fubject to the depredations of thefe animals. No fooner do they fcent the full-eared corn, than they make their way, if poffible, to it;—no fence proves a fufficient reftraint;—the nightly watch is placed in vain;—and fcarce a ftalk efcapes their ravages.

The foil in this quarter confifts of a cold watery clay, which fo imbibes the moifture, that the crops of corn, and even of hay, except in dry fummers, but poorly repay the
farmer's

farmer's toil. The oak alone is its boaſt;
which proudly ſpreads its nervous branches,
and grows for the defence of Britain.

Lindhurſt, which is ten miles from Southampton, is ſituated in the heart of the foreſt.
It is a pleaſant agreeable village, and ſtands
on the declivity of a hill. It once could
boaſt of having a monarch for an inhabitant;
at preſent the houſe which was the royal
reſidence, is that of the duke of Glouceſter,
who is lord chief warden, and ranger of the
foreſt. It is a plain old faſhioned brick manſion, with little or no ground adjoining to it.
The greateſt convenience attending it is the
ſtables, which are roomy and commodious.
They ſtand oppoſite to the houſe, which is
without any court before it, or lodge, con-
ſequently expoſed to the duſt of the road;
and has rather the appearance of being the
reſidence of a gentleman farmer, than the
ſummer retreat of one of the princes of the
blood.

But if its conveniences are few, its advantages of another nature are great.—
Standing

Standing on an eminence, it commands a complete profpect of Southampton River, and of the fea.—The view extends likewife into the county of Suffex.—Stony Crofs on the left, and, over the foreft, to the woody fcreens of fir William Heathcote, with the foft diftances of the remoteft parts of Hampfhire.

In the village of Lindhurft conftant pre- parations are made for the accommodation of gentlemen who come to hunt in the fo- reft. Nor can any place be better fuited to the fport, there being but few farms, to what there are in the counties of Hertford, Bedford, and fome others. Neither do the fportfmen run fuch rifque of their necks as in moft other hunting counties, as there are not many fences or ditches to obftruct their courfe, and confequently few dan- gerous leaps to be taken.

We read in the annals of England, that the tract of country now denominated the New Foreft, and which is at leaft fifty miles in circumference, originally abounded with
towns

towns and villages, in which were no lefs than thirty-fix parifh churches. But it was laid wafte, and the inhabitants driven from their houfes and eftates by William the Firft, in order to gratify his *penchant* for the pleafures of the chace. The diftrefs which this Norman conquerer thereby wantonly brought upon his new fubjects, feems however to have been in fome degree retaliated on his own family; for two of his fons, and a grandfon, loft their lives on the very fpot. His fon Richard was killed by a peftilential blaft;—William Rufus, as is well known, was flain by an arrow fhot by Sir Walter Tyrrel at a ftag;—and Henry, his grandfon, while purfuing his game, was caught by the hair of his head, which had entangled in the bough of a tree, and there fufpended till he died.

From Lindhurft we kept the left hand road to Lymington; and paffed Fox Leafe, the feat of Lady Jennings Clerke. We were not fortunate enough to be able to procure a fight of the infide of this villa, her ladyfhip being there, and having company.—
The

The external appearance of it is neat, and the ground that furrounds it pleafant, though not fuperb.

Burleigh Lodge, and Cuffnells, the feat of George Rofe, Efq. are near Lindhurft; befides which there are many other agreeable fpots; fome the fummer refidences, others the hunting boxes, of the proprietors.

The road ftill continued its courfe through a woody range that formed noble groups, while a gradual light, darting through the thinner branches in the diftance, caught fome open fpace, where lightly touching the neighbouring cot, whofe thatch, with moffy weeds overgrown, foftly blended with the huge oak boughs that overfhadowed the roof, formed a pleafing effect;—at the fame time the mouldering fpire of Brokenhurft, clinging to the elm and yew, juft fhows its fhaded pile. The fore ground thus laid in fhadow, with a fmall piece of water rufhing at its foot, with a fingle light upon the diftant cottage, and grazing herd, almoft formed a picture of itfelf; but when the

fhy

ſhy ſpire, darting from the firſt diſtance, appeared ſhaded by a flying cloud, it was a perfect compoſition for a rural picture.—The laſt diſtance was fraught with one of thoſe purple glows that the ſetting ſun ſo freely diſplays on a clear evening, when, exhaling the vapour of the moiſtened earth, it ſo charmingly blends each diſtant hill and copſe with its ærial perſpective.

On the right is the manſion of Edward Morant, Eſq. ſituated on the very ſummit of one of the pleaſanteſt hills in the foreſt. Two avenues lead to it from Brokenhurſt. The park is plainly laid out;—the houſe equal to any modern one for convenience:—the entrance is grand,—and the rooms are ſpacious and lofty.—The poſſeſſor, when he began to build, ſeems to have had a deſire to render it uſeful as well as elegant.—The offices lie behind the houſe, as do the gardens. We much regretted the want of a piece of water before this manſion, as ſuch an addition would render it a compleat and deſirable reſidence; but this deficiency is in ſome meaſure ſupplied by a ſmall ſtream

which

which croffes the bottom of the park, and though not feen from the houfe, has a defirable effect.

Brokenhurft is one of thofe remote fpots where real pleafure may be enjoyed.—It is an agreeable diftance from Lymington, and a morning's ride from Southampton, acrofs a floping woody country. Several very refpectable perfons refide in this place and the adjacent parts, and a fociability feems to reign among them, free from that fcandal and bickering which too frequently difturb the tranquillity of many villages.

Rifing another elevation of the foreft, we got a clear and diftinct view of the Ifle of Wight.—On our right-hand continued the fame range of woods we had paffed as we came from Lindhurft; on the other fide a wide defert heath encountered our fight.— We paffed on through another fmall village, and then entered a grand burft of landfcape;—a rugged rock formed the right fide fcreen;—the towering boughs that hung on the oppofite fide of the road drooped

E their

their branches almoft on the withered fern which courted the gravelly bank ;—from this, a gentle declivity of trees fell to the water's edge, that winding round two woody promontories break the ftiff appearance of the oppofite fhore, and terminate at the bridge.—At this diftance the formality of the buildings on the quays had not fufficient ftrength to leffen the picturefque appearance.—Another piece of water, taking a gentle fweep round the baths of Lymington, difcharges itfelf into the fea.—The Ifle of Wight terminates the view ;—though its chalky cliffs have not fufficient power to pleafe, they may attract the eye.

Lymington, though a fmall, is a very convenient feaport ; its diftance from Southampton is eighteen miles, through the pleafanteft part of the New Foreft. Part of the town ftands on an eminence, and leads to the quays, which are fpacious and convenient. Ships of confiderable burthen fail from this place ; efpecially fome that are employed in the coal trade. Oppofite Lymington river are the well known rocks, called

called the Needles, a defcription of which will be given when we fpeak of the Ifle of Wight.

It is an ancient borough, governed by a mayor, aldermen, and burgeffes, without any limited number. But it does not redound much to the credit of this ancient corporation, that when his majefty deigned to vifit their town, during his late ftay at Lindhurft, not even a cold collation was prepared for his reception, notwithftanding they had previous notice of the intended honour ; a *neglect*, to call it by no harfher name, that his majefty's condefcenfion, affability, and goodnefs of heart, were far from deferving.

Were it not that our plan is rather to confine ourfelves to a defcription of the picturefque views of nature and the effect they have on the imagination, than in making obfervations on men and manners, we could mention other anecdotes of a fimilar nature ; but, for the foregoing reafon, fhall content ourfelves with felecting from them the following.—

E 2

When

When his majesty, on his late summer
excursion, was at Southampton, having en-
quired of one of the body corporate of that
town which way the wind was, and received
for answer that it was *south-west*; another of
the robed brothers put in, with an infolent
familiarity, not at all befitting the perfonage to whom it was addreffed, " I believe
it is not *saw-weft*, your majefty, but *nor-
efe*." The reader, who is acquainted with
the dialect of the country, will beft be able
to difcern from it the vulgarity of the
fpeaker, and the indecency of the fpeech.
We were pleafed to obferve that the countenance of the moft gracious of fovereigns,
exhibited greater expreffion of pity and contempt, than of difpleafure.

We could not difcover any thing of antiquity at or near Lymington, and met with
but one circumftance worth relating. The
trade for cattle between this place and the
ifles of Jerfey and Alderney, is very confiderable, and the manner of fhipping and
of landing them rather curious. Having
faftened a rope round the horns of the beaft,
the

the failors hoift his head to the height of four or five feet from the ground, till only the hind hoofs touch the plank that extends from the fhore to the fhip. And in this manner is he dragged on board; the failors all the while endeavouring to accelerate his motion by twifting his tail. In this attitude the embarking beaft cuts a droll figure, and never fails to attract a great number of fpectators.

The Portfmouth family take their fecond title from this place, the eldeft fon being vifcount Lymington. The people of the town boaft of the frequent vifits they receive from this noble houfe, who are not only well known here, but as well refpected.

As our route, on our return from the Ifle of Wight, whither we are haftening, will lie through this place, in order to take the New Foreft in another direction, fhould any thing occur worthy of obfervation, we fhall then notice it.

E 3   SECTION

SECTION III.

ON leaving Lymington, we coafted the fhore which we had feen the preceding evening; but had it not now in our power to attract from it thofe pleafurable moments we had then done. The morning was heavy, and the fky lowered during the greateft part of the day.

At the extremity of the road we turned up to the village of Boldre, which has to boaft the refidence of the Rev. Mr. Gilpin; the productions of whofe elegant pen are well known. It is a fmall village, furrounded by firs and oaks, and has feveral gentlemen for its inhabitants.

From hence we paffed on through another fmall village, to Beaulieu Heath, as it is termed by thofe who refide near it; but we found it to be another extremity of the foreft. The feat of fir John D'Oyley ftands at one corner of it, whofe houfe and park, though boafting of nothing more than

we

we generally meet with, help to relieve a barren turf-dug heath.

Turning down the right-hand road a little beyond D'Oyley houfe, it took us to the iron mills. Thefe once profitable engines have fhared the fate which generally attends any concern where there are a great number of proprietors. Difputes continually arifing, the mills are faid to have been reduced by them to their prefent defolate condition. Formerly the iron ore received from the Ifle of Wight was fufficient to keep them conftantly at work. After that they were fupplied from Lancafhire, on account of the fuperior quality. But the difagreements before mentioned having put an entire ftop to them, they are now fuffered to moulder into duft.

The falt works along this coaft furnifh no inconfiderable branch of traffic. At one place, in the neighbourhood of Lymington, five pans are continually working; and many more along the coaft to Fawley.

From

From the mills, we once more gained the heath, and took the road to Beaulieu. But a very heavy ftorm, which had threatened us ever fince we left Lymington, now commencing, we pofted with all fpeed over the heath. We had not, however, proceeded far, before fome peafants, who were gathering turf, called out to us to ftop immediately; and upon coming up informed us, that if we had gone a few fteps farther we fhould have plunged into a bog, to the great hazard of our own, and our horfes' lives. We would, therefore, advife every traveller, when they pafs over this heath, or any other where there may be a fufpicion of meeting with bogs, or loofe beds of clay, which are nearly as bad, that they would by no means endeavour to crofs in any direction but by the high road, or at leaft where the track of wheels are to be traced.

We thanked the men for their kind attention; and the rain ftill continuing to pour down with unabated fury on our heads, we haftened towards Beaulieu; but St. Leonards, or, as fome call it, Beaulieu

Manor,

Manor, lying nearer, and fome remains of
antiquity being to be found there, we made
for that place.. We here met with a wel-
come retreat from the ftorm at a homely
farm-houfe, and were entertained in a moft
friendly manner by the hofpitable owner
of it.

The principal remaining part of the
abbey of St. Leonard, confifts of two high
walls that feem to have terminated the
cloifter. Thefe now conftitute the ends
of a modern-built thatched barn. The
other parts are nearly extinct, and are converted into a pig-ftye. The ruins being fo
inconfiderable, and fo defaced by the beams
of wood, and thatched out-houfes, refting
upon them, fcarce a veftige of its former
beauty remains, to afford a fingle point of
view in which a pleafing drawing could be
made of it.

The wind having difperfed the heavy
clouds, and cleared again the fky, and
there being nothing more in this place
worthy of obfervation, we took leave of
our

our kind hoft, and purfued our courfe to Beaulieu through the fouth-eaft part of the New Foreft.

Here they have begun to diveft the foreft of a part of its grandeur, by cutting down a confiderable quantity of its hardy vete-rans—the noble oaks; but fo delightful are the avenues which here and there break an opening to the Ifle of Wight, that every curve delights the traveller's eye. A woody fide-fcreen ftill keeps to your right hand the whole of the way to Beaulieu, which is five miles from St. Leonard's.

There are feveral falt works near the mouth of Beaulieu river, which employ a great number of poor inhabitants. The village, or town, of Beaulieu is agreeably difpofed in one ftreet, and lies at the foot of feveral hills that gradually fkirt the banks of the river, over which a continued verdure reigns; fo that from Beaulieu mills it ap-pears more like a garden than common woods.

Some

Some relicks of antiquity are ftill vifible
where the abbey once ftood; but they are
fo few, that it is impoffible to combine
the fcattered remains into any point of
fight that would form a picture, or give a
likenefs of the place. There is a wall in
fome degree of prefervation, which feems to
have furrounded the abbey, and which
muft, judging from the prefent appearance
of it, have been more than a mile in circumference.

Part of the old chapel is applied to the
purpofes of a cork-warehoufe. It is fituated near the walls which encompafs the
joint feat of the duke of Montague and
lord Beaulieu. This ancient houfe, which
was erected about the reign of king John,
appears to be ftill unfhaken by the hand
of Time; nor has the daring ivy touched
its ftony fides. The building is very ftiff,
but pleafing to the view, without any further pretentions to external beauty than
merely fimplicity and neatnefs.

The infide of this feat is lefs curious than
the outfide. The whole flooring is of oak,
and

and quite perfect; the ſtaircaſe, wainſcot, and beams, are of the ſame wood. The duke of Montague has not viſited it theſe thirty years; nor are we ſurprized at his abſence, the houſe not having, at preſent, a ſingle convenience for a family. It is ſurrounded by a ditch, and has four draw-bridges over it, that communicate with the park, which is a beautiful piece of ground, well watered and wooded. In the church-yard, anciently belonging to the monaſ-tery, there ſtill appear the relicks of a few Saxon characters, as inſcriptions on the tombs; but they are very much injured and defaced by time and the weather. The monaſtery itſelf, that is, the two ſmall remaining walls, being at this time a nur-ſery for bees, we were thereby prevented from making a minuter ſearch into the ſtate of it.

From Beaulieu you paſs another turn of the river towards Fawley, which ſhines in every pictureſque ſplendour: and this laſts till you arrive at the ſummit of the hill that enters again the New Foreſt. Here let me
renew

renew the caution I before gave the unwary
traveller, not to crofs the heath without
due attention. Before he takes the de-
ceptious tracks of the horfe's hoof, or even
the muddy ruts of a cart, for his guide over
the unfure fod, let him notice well the hand-
poft;—efpecially if the declining fun throws
its lengthening fhadows from the thorny
bufhes.

For noblenefs, as a burft of landfcape, the
view from this hill is perhaps as pleafing as
it is uncommon; and the only deficiency we
could perceive, was the want of fome bold
promontory to the left, inftead of a dreary
heath. On the right-hand, the Ifle of Wight,,
gently floping from its wonted heights, juft
left fpace enough between it and the oppofite
fhore of Stokes Bay to fhow the fwelling
fails that fweep along the Spit. In front, at
the diftance of about a mile and a half acrofs
the heath, a plantation of oak gradually
declines into the valley that opens to the fea,
and coming within the general bounds of
the horizon, foftens the harfher appearance
of

of the black furze that forms the fore-
ground.

The road to Fawley, which is five miles
from Beaulieu, is directly opposite to the
gate that limits the boundary of the foreft.
The heath, as juft obferved, is covered with
furze; and, though it lies high, has many
bogs on it. The preceding day having
proved very rainy, the part of the road we
were to purfue was utterly impaffable for foot
paffengers, and nearly fo for horfes. Thofe
we rode on, at every ftep they took, funk
almoft up to the girths in a heavy clay and
water; and though the road, from the gate
at which we entered to another part of the
woods lefs fwampy, was only two miles in
length, we were at leaft an hour and a half
in paffing it.

We were however foon compenfated for
the trouble and fatigue we had undergone
in getting through this fwamp. The Ifle of
Wight now became a weftern boundary,
and appeared in all its fplendour; the neareft
fhores preffed hard on our firft diftance;

and

and Cowes road, forming a recefs, was relieved by the hills near St. Catherine's.

Our deftination being for Eagle Hurft, the
feat of lord Carhampton, we paffed Fawley on the left, and proceeded along the
brow of a furly heath. This building is an
excellent land mark, and elegant in its outward appearance. From the top of the
tower, it commands a very extenfive view
of the ifland and the oppofite fhores to the
eaft and north; and from its weftern fide,
the major part of the foreft; where Redbridge and Langford Hills are very confpicuous. Southampton and its river have a
capital appearance. The fouth weft profpect
prefents the Hills of Lymington, and the
country towards Chrift-church.

Eagle Hurft, or as it is generally named
by the inhabitants of the coaft, Luttrell's
Folly, is built clofe to the fhore, and near
the point on which ftands Calfhot Caftle.
The building is very whimfical, but neat
and agreeable to the fight. On the top of
it a round tower is erected, which was originally

ginally intended to have a full view over the
fouthern fhores of the Ifle of Wight; but unfortunately the director or architect forgot
that the ground on which it ftands is not of
an equal height with the intervening mountains on the ifland. The portico has a pleafant appearance, and is very convenient.

The infide of the houfe, or caftle if the
reader fo pleafes, (for it mounts a few
pieces of cannon on its battlements) is both
commodious and elegant in the extreme.
The ground floor has two parlours. On
the firft floor there is a handfome and fpacious drawing-room. The *baffo-relievos* that
are fixed in the walls are executed in a maf-
terly manner, and well felected;—nor is the
judgment of its noble proprietor lefs confpicuous in his felection of a Venus and
Cupid, a beautiful picture from the Italian
fchool, which hangs in the beft bed-room.
We could not help regretting that his lordfhip has not a collection ; as from this picture, and a few fcarce etchings by Francifco
Londonio, of Milan, we might expect it to
be well chofen.

But

But to return to the drawing-room.
We feldom fee fo much neatnefs as reigns
here. A curious glafs lock is affixed to its
door on a fingular conftruction. The furniture is plain, and the walls are of a plain
paper, with gold and filver bordering. A
bed-room on the fame floor is as neat and
convenient as the drawing-room. On the
fecond floor is a dreffing-room and bed-
chamber, with every elegance that denotes
judgment.

From this, a well-ftaircafe conducted us
to the top of the round tower, where
we enjoyed one of the moft extenfive views
Hampfhire can boaft. The kitchens, except
being damp in winter, are equally convenient with the other parts of the houfe.
Several fubterraneous paffages lead from
the area to a number of marquees, to which
the family retire when the turbulence of the
weather renders a refidence in the houfe
difagreeable. In thefe tents there are feveral beds, and alfo a kitchen. The houfe
being fmall, thefe retreats are both cool and
agreeable. At their back ftands a yew
hedge,

hedge, which protects them from the severity of the north and north-west winds. From hence another paſſage underground leads to a bathing-houſe on the beach. All theſe retreats are well bricked and floored; but ſo very wet at times, that they are impaſſable.

Calſhot Caſtle, which lies on this neck of land, has nothing in its appearance to recommend it to attention. It is of a round form, with a draw-bridge, and a few buildings for the garriſon, which conſiſts of invalids. It was built by Henry the Eighth, for the defence of Southampton; but at preſent appears to be of little ſtrength, and of leſs conſequence.

We now returned to Fawley for the night, a pleaſant ride of about three miles; the oppoſite ſhores of the river, which are a perfect garden, continually burſting on the ſight. Fawley is a ſmall but very pleaſant town. There are a few ſalt works here, but not of ſo much conſideration as thoſe adjoining to Lymington. Nothing of antiquity lies nearer to it than Beaulieu.

Mr.

Mr. Drummond has a feat fituated about a mile from Fawley, and nearly the fame diftance from the fhore. From the back of it are very extenfive views up and down the river; but that from the front of it is chiefly confined to the grounds before the houfe.

The infide of the manfion is fpacious and elegant. The rooms are lofty. A moft noble dining-room and drawing-room, with a parlour, a library, and other apartments, are on the ground floor. When we entered the library, we obferved, over the fire-place, a piece, which we fuppofed to be by Rubens. It is one of thofe capital landfcapes that were engraved by Bolfvert. The fore ground of it is rather crowded, but the colouring and diftance are equal to any thing the pencil of that great artift ever produced. We expected to have found more pictures, form this fpecimen of Mr. Drummond's judgment; but could only fee two fmall fea pieces accompanying this noble *chef d'œuvre* of the mafter.

On

On the firſt floor, which conſiſts of bed-
chambers, the rooms are equally ſpacious
and neat. The idea of convenience ſeems
to have ſpread itſelf all over the houſe.
Nor is the ſecond floor leſs deſirable than
the firſt. Theſe two floors contain fourteen
bed-rooms, beſides dreſſing rooms &c. &c.
The hall at the entrance of the houſe ſup-
ports its roof with a few pillars quite plain.
The offices are adjoining to the houſe, and
are ſuch as we generally find attached
to gentlemens' ſeats: The grounds round
the houſe are well laid out, both for pleaſure
and convenience. At the bottom of the
park, near the water, is a farm, in which
there appears to be little, except convenience, to render it worthy of notice.

From Mr. Drummond's we entered again
the turnpike road, and purſued our way
to Hythe, a ſmall town lying about ſix miles
off. The road to this place is through one
of the pleaſanteſt ſpots near Hampton, for
a morning's excurſion. The foreſt, in many
parts, ſweeps to the water's edge. It however preſents nothing very different from
what

what we had hitherto feen. Till we arrived at Hythe, it was a plain ftrait road, with a continual profpect of the oppofite fhores. We there gained a totally different afpect of Southampton, from a piece of broken ground, bounded by a few foreft plants, under whofe branches we had a moft picturefque view of the town and fhipping.

The fcale was too large to be circumfcribed in a fmall drawing, and too grand for any thing lefs than a picture. A gentle declivity of the hill fwept round a few fhrubs that gradually declined the fteep ;—a newly mown clover field, with the fun catching full on it, and on it alone, bounded the fore ground ;—while the river, variegating its fhades, terminated with Hampton and its diftance in an entire fhadow. But though Southampton appeared the grandeft object in the diftance, it was too far off to bring into a compafs fmall enough for this work, without ruining its compofition.

Hythe is a fmall fifhing town, whofe chief dependance is on its oppofite neigh-

bour,

bour, Southampton. A few ſhips, and thoſe
of no conſiderable burthen, are built here;
and we muſt add, their conſtruction is attended with every inconvenience that can
belong to a ſhore. A continual bed of mud
extends itſelf from Calſhot Caſtle to Redbridge, and renders landing, even at high
water, very diſagreeable. When the tide
ebbs, in moſt parts it is nearly an im-
poſſibility to get to ſea at all. We rode
along the ſhore a little way towards Eling,
but were prevented by the continual beds
of mud from going farther.

We therefore turned again into the Redbridge road, and purſued our route through
a moſt luxurious continuance of oaks and
aſhes which ſkirt the road. We cannot
leave this route from Fawley, without re-
minding the viſitors of Hampton, that when
they are deſirous of a pleaſant and variegated excurſion, it will be hardly poſſible
for them to find a more ſheltered, pleaſing,
and good road, than that from Southampton
over Redbridge to Eling and Hythe. And
if they wiſh for an aquatic excurſion back

to

to Hampton, they may proceed from thence;
it being only three miles acrofs; whereas
by the road way it is twelve miles.

Being now defirous of traverfing the fhores
of Southampton River by water, we fent our
horfes back, and proceeded from the mouth
of the river Beft, along the fouthern fhore.
At Redbridge, the Beft joins the water of
Hampton, and fo powerfully does it predominate, that at ebb tide it almoft frefhens
the falt water. The Itching and Hamble
rivers likewife blend their ftreams into the
water of Hampton; fo that bathing in it
can fcarcely, in our opinion, be confidered
as bathing in *falt* water.

But to return. We intended, as has juft
been faid, to fail along the fhores of the river
and obferve its different appearances. Our
voyage would have been very pleafant, could
we have kept one fhore clofe, while the other
might keep its diftance; but we were exceedingly difgufted at the continual fhoals
of mud that obliged us to confine ourfelves
almoft to mid-channel.

F 4   Eling

Eling fpire, from the water, has a pleafant appearance among its woody banks;
but a quantity of ftiff paling, painted white,
proved a difgufting contraft to the har-
monizing bank, and clinging fhrub.

A beautiful vegetation fpreads itfelf along
the fhore towards Hythe; but not having
the advantage of a rifing or a fetting fun, we
loft the greateft part of its beauties. The
glare of a mid-day fun on the plants, hurts
the eye;—nor was the movement of the tide
fmooth enough to catch its variegated fhades.
On a fine clear evening, when fcarcely a
breath of air floats on the furface of the
gliding ftream, we have often obferved one
wave, carelefsly rolling to the coming tide,
catch the fun's reflections on fome evening
cloud,

And ftain its mirror with the wood's foft hues;

giving to the admirers and watchers of her
motions, every tranfport that a breaft, fuf-
ceptible of picturefque fcenes, can poffibly
feel from the conjunction of all the beauties
that Nature boafts. We are perfuaded, that
when the imagination of a picturefque ob-

ferver

ferver is fired at a combination of pleafing objects, thus fuddenly prefenting themfelves,
they afford the higheft pleafure the heart is
capable of experiencing.—But was dame
Nature continually to prefent her grandeft
objects to our view, we fhould foon grow
infenfible to them; and all thofe feelings
which adorn the mind, would lofe much of
their vigour and efficacy.

The fhore ftill bore the fame afpect all the
way to Hythe. From the water, this town
has a pleafant appearance;—nor is the dock
ungrateful to the fight. Little difference
in the view is feen along the fhore to Mr.
Drummond's; the elegance of which from
the river diminifhes confiderably. Nothing
of novelty is perceptible till we reach Calfhot Caftle. From this fpot Hampton appears very diminutive;—nor does any place
but Cowes road fhow to advantage. Eagle Hurft lofes its noble appearance;—and
even the fhips at Spithead are not diftinctly
to be difcerned by the naked eye.

Stretching over to the oppofite fhore, we
made up the harbour. Wood chiefly accompanies

companies the banks of the river along this fide as well as the other. Governor Hornby's houfe was the only manfion that broke the view till we came to the mouth of Hamble river. The tide running ftrongly out, we were not able to land.

Hamble Church has a pleafing appearance from the water, and agreeably relieves the fight. At this village there was formerly a priory of Ciftercian monks, dedicated to St. Andrew, which became a cell to the abbey of Tirone in France, and was at length given to New College in Oxford. We intended to have landed here, but were prevented by the current; and night approaching, we ftood out again, when we repaffed a continuation of the fame fcenes.

The fort of Netley Abbey makes but an inconfiderable appearance from the water. Itching river was our next principal object. This we ferried up. The village of Itching confifts of a few houfes that ftray along its fhore. Woody fcreens bind its right hand, while a more open fpace lies on its left.

We

We found but few things worth attention till we arrived at Wood Mill, near South Stoneham, where there is a lock which admits the barges going to Winchester, and is the only navigable passage. The back part of Mr. Sloane's house commands a view of the whole river, itself appearing very conspicuous. We returned down the opposite banks, and passed Denis's or St. Dionysius's priory. From hence general Stibbert's house has every prospect that can be wished for. Nothing further presented itself to claim notice on the opposite shore, except Sydney Farm, and the houses on Pear-tree Green. Leaving the river, we now passed the point, and landed at Hampton quay.

A desire of visiting Broadlands, the seat of lord Palmerston, led us next to Romsey. The road from Southampton to that place strikes off near the polygon, to 'the right, over the common. On this road the New Forest, which lies to the left, appears in every grandeur possible till we pass the heath. His lordship's woods hence skirt the road on both sides. A disagreeable plantation

of

of firs prefent themfelves at its entrance, but are foon relieved by the more pliable faplings of the oak and the afh. Thefe woods entirely formed our left hand fcreens, while the adjacent hills of the foreft terminated in a delightful and fertile valley.

Near the five mile ftone, on the left, lies Mr. Fletcher's houfe. It is a fpacious building, and, viewed from the road, feems to boaft a venerable antiquity. Though low, it commands a fine clear view of the furrounding country. The river Beft runs clofe to the grounds; and the profpect of the continual woods and promontories that verge into the valley, gives a fimplicity to the fcene, together with every beauty that can enliven the imagination.

Verging to the left, we had an opening to the fpire of Romfey church.—Of this edifice, and the antiquities of Romfey, we intend to fpeak more fully when we treat of the northern parts of our tour. Our defign at this time being more particularly to take a view of lord Palmerfton's feat, we we fhall confine ourfelves at prefent to that.

The noble proprietor, much to his credit, permits the inhabitants of the adjacent parts to fhare in the pleafures of his grounds. Several walks interfect the park, which are conftantly reforted to by the neighbouring gentry. The fpace before the front of the houfe is elegant in the extreme, and regularly planted with pleafing, but fmall fhrubberies. The lodge is fimply plain, and difcovers the refined tafte of its owner; nor could we perceive in any one of the apartments, or any article of the furniture, any trait of a want of that refined tafte.— Elegance and neatnefs, directed by judgment, predominate through the whole manfion.

The houfe is a fquare building;—the porch fupported by four ftately pillars, with a parlour on each fide;—the windows high and convenient.—But when the inquifitive traveller, allured from the road by the external appearance, takes a view of the

inside

infide, he then finds that the beauties and conveniences within, are far fuperior to thofe without.

The hall, which is fquare and fpacious, is adorned with a few ftatues. A Venus *de Medicis*; an Apollo; a drunken Bacchante and dancing Faun; embellifh the receffes. A few others, fmall, but correct, are placed over the doors.

From hence we entered the right-hand parlour; an elegant lofty room, with well-fuited furniture. The dining-room is alfo of a good fize, and complete in all points. But when we were fhown into the library, we were then fully convinced of the juftice of the encomium we beftowed on this houfe, when we began our account of it. The combination of his lordfhip's collection of pictures, which indeed are but few, heightened the fatisfaction we had at firft received.

A waterfall by Ruyfdal, and that in his beft manner, was almoft loft to our fight, by being hung fo high. The colouring of
this

this piece is in his ufual ftile of foftnefs and
harmony; but too much ftudied. The flying clouds in mid-day, are in his firft manner; a littlenefs, however, appears in the
waterfall, from its being carried over a number of rocks in fmall ftreams. We regretted
the want of a body of water in the fore-
ground, to form the principal light; but
this defect was fully compenfated by its
other beauties.

A large picture by one of the Flemifh
fchool, is wonderfully correct; the fubject a merry-making. Two landfcapes by
Claude; the diftant colouring foft and pleafant. The fore-grounds of thefe pictures
are not unlike the touch of Patel; but the
diftances are fo brightly coloured, and in
fo warm a ftile, that we pronounce them
Claude's;—more experienced connoiffeurs
we leave to their own judgment.

Two pieces of Sir Jofhua's prefented themfelves to us, as we entered the door. The
firft was the children in the wood; a charming, foft, and beautiful colouring; the defign

fign is as delicate and fpirited, as the colouring is chafte. The fubject was eafily
diftinguifhable by the bilberry-ftained lips of
the dormant child. The expreffion of the
other child, and fleepy eye, for which the
pencil of Sir Jofhua is famed, almoft de-
prived us of the pleafure that we ought to
have viewed the other pictures with.

Its companion, a much frefher, though
equally capital performance, was a Venus,
with an attendant, chiding a Cupid, who,
affected by his mother's lecture, ftands dif-
confolately weeping. This performance, we
could not help remarking, feemed to be
carried to the higheft pitch the art of paint-
ing can admit of. The portrait of the
attendant in the back ground is moft ad-
mirable. Of all the faces that ever the
pencil gave birth to, we fincerely think this
is the moft perfect. So excellent an idea
never entered the mind of a painter as
that which feems to have infpired the pencil of Sir Jofhua when this portrait was
produced by it. The ftriking light on the
right fide is exquifite; while the reverfe
lays

lays in one of the fineſt half tints ever ex-
preſſed by a Rubens or a Vandyke.

A picture by another artiſt of the Italian
ſchool, and a ceiling by the ſame, are well
executed. Several other pieces, ſelected with
equal judgment, grace the library. A few
baſſo relievos and ſtatues alſo adorn the
ſides of it; but above all, a capital piece of
a Venus couchant, which is placed on a ſlab.
The taſte and execution of this piece of
marble, aſſiſted by the trueſt ſymmetry in
all its proportions, and in point of per-
ſonal beauty equally capital, render it a
complete piece of the maſter. Another lies
under the ſlab, but is far inferior to the
former.

The great convenience of this room, joined to its pleaſantneſs, and the view from it,
make it a very deſirable room for ſitting in,
and it is therefore much frequented by his
lordſhip. From this room we paſſed into
another equally elegant; which alſo contained book-caſes and a few pictures.

After having viewed the remaining rooms on the ground floor, we proceeded up-ftairs. Here we were again gratified with a voluptuous treat of a few more pictures. In an elegant and fpacious apartment, which we fuppofed to be a dining-room, were a pair of capital landfcapes by Marlow. The colouring of them is in his beft manner. A prevalent harmony runs through the whole. The fcenes are in the Italian ftile. The principal one is a bridge; a river the other. Two pictures, very like the ftile of Mr. Farrington, are equally capital. Some cattle pieces (but none by Bergham, that we could fee) with a Woverman's, and a few others, fill the room.

The bed-rooms are convenient and neat in the extreme; particularly one, in which we were informed lady Palmerfton's fifter flept. To give a detail of every beauty, convenience, and elegance that this houfe abounds with, internally and externally, would much exceed the limits of our work.

The views from the houfe are pleafing
and

and picturefque. From the library before-
mentioned, we entered the back grounds
and gardens. The new ftone bridge over
the river, appears from this part to add
frefh luftre to the fcene; and is admirably
well contrived to form an extremity to the
park. The river Beft paffing through the
park, forms a pleafant and interefting fub-
qually tafty with the houfe and other parts;
ject in the grounds. The gardens are e-
and indeed for a combination of elegance,
judgment, and neatnefs, Broadlands has
fcarcely its equal.

G 2   SECTION

SECTION IV.

THE evening drawing on, we left this agreeable place, and set out for Redbridge, to spend the night. Little that was novel presented itself as we went on, till we looked down upon Redbridge from a wood. The river of Southampton and the Isle of Wight, as in general they do here, closed the evening scene.

The road through Longford to White Parish Hill was our next route. Here we struck into the forest at Totten, and explored the most northern boundaries of it. The woody screens of the Romsey road from Hampton now appeared on the right; while Stony Cross bounded our first left hand distance; and Ower appeared as the nearest village on the high road. The spire of Romsey Church had a desirable effect, from the number of breaks that presented it to us. Mr. Fletcher's house was continually in view for four miles. Lord Palmerston's was not always so discernible; the

uninterrupted

uninterrupted range of woods that inter-
vened, overtopping each other, fcarcely permitted his lordfhip's houfe, from this point
of view, to prefent its elegance to our fight.

An unvarying famenefs continued for the
greateft part of the way till we came near
Poulton's, formerly the feat of the right
honourable Hans Stanley, now of Welbore
Ellis, Efq. No part of this houfe can be
feen from the road we were in, the avenue
leading to it being entirely furrounded by
firs and other fmall plantations, which are
frequent in this part of the foreft, and appear to be cultivated by art.

The infide of Poulton Houfe has nothing
out of the common line to boaft of. It is
however furrounded with beautiful and extenfive lawns, through which winds a fer-
pentine river.

From this place we kept the right hand
road, and foon entered a new fcene, it being barren, and void of thofe beautiful
fore-grounds the foreft fo frequently pre-

G 3   fents ;

fents. But here, Nature fmiling in the diftance, feemed to defpife one of her barren
productions. A moft luxurious cover,
fpreading itfelf along the ridge of our firft
diftance, gradually defcended in a fweep below, on a difagreeable uniform hill. Above
the firft wood, a grand mountain relieved the
humble foliage of the irregular oaks. From
the weftern extremity, another copfe reared
its flender ftems, and fweeping down a diftant dell, loft itfelf in the entangled branches
of the firft diftance. A few other broken
hills from the eaft alfo took their curve
down to the woods ;—while the fetting fun,
blending its laft rays with a few diftant hills
which terminated the picture, gave fpirit and
beauty to every tree that joined them. But
when we caft our eyes on the overgrown
fhrubby heath that furrounded our fore-
ground, we could not help obferving the def-
picable appearance which the planted pines
cut. Their ftiffnefs, joined to the barrennefs
of foliage around, fo offended the fight, that
the fpot we ftood on feemed as a foil to the
fublimity of the voluntary effufions of Nature.

Difgufted

Difgufted at the contraft, we fancied we
faw *Nature* looking down with contempt on
the forming hand of *Art* that had raifed the
firs; and at the fame time were led to pity
the endeavours of man when he attempts
to heighten the charms of Nature by the in-
effectual aids of Art. We often hear paint-
ers declaim againft Nature's ever being able
to combine objects for a picture. But if I
dare hazard fuch an affertion, I would fay,
I am firmly of opinion that never painter
pourtrayed a landfcape in fuch a ftile of ex-
cellence as may be feen in many parts of
the New Foreft and the Ifle of Wight. As
the heath grew blacker, fo the diftance appeared lively and dazzling. Thus we often
fee the diftant copfe, inveloped in the greateft degree of luxuriance that Nature can
poffibly fpread, endeavouring to foften the
hard lines of an ungrateful foil, where the
bleak north-eaft wind

Scatters the remnants of his furly blafts.

Nor was a fcene we faw the fame evening
at the boundary of a wood near Longford,
lefs interefting than the foregoing. A group
of cows, with a few fheep, returning to their

nightly

nightly afylum, throwing up as they went on, a cloud of duft againft the wood;—the fun at the fame time juft verging and tinting the fummits of a few oaks;—had a fine effect. The herdfmen in the rear were in a fuperb and fofter colouring by the inceffant effects the cattle occafioned. Two of the foremoft, with fome fheep, were perfectly difcernible; the reft gradually foftened away.

Longford is thirteen miles from Southampton, in a pleafant healthy part of the foreft, fituated on the floping cavity of a way-worn hill, furrounded by grand verdure, and overhanging fhrubs.—Mr. Eyre has a feat here; and his fon alfo has one, which commands very extenfive views of the parts of Hampfhire bordering on the county of Wilts.

About two miles beyond Longford we had feveral delightful views, where the woods formed fore-grounds, and the diftances were equal to any in thefe parts. One in particular engaged our attention at the

the turnpike between Longford and White Parifh Hill; the other about a mile on this side of the laft-mentioned place.

Nothing further, worthy of obfervation, fell in our way, till we arrived at White Parifh Hill. Deer Park, where captain Eyre refides, is a pleafant retired fpot, poffeffed of fufficient charms for any private family.

But when we had reached the fummit of the hill, we were quite enraptured. Such a fcene opened upon us as is feldom ever feen. —Salifbury fpire prefents itfelf from a well-topped fhrubbery that ranges down the weft-ern fide of Alderbury Common, and breaks a diftance, which otherwife would rather cloy, than afford the exquifite pleafure every fpec-tator muft now view it with. The ap-pearance of the fpire is charmingly relieved by the plains. Of the city in which this elegant ftructure ftands, we fhall fpeak more fully hereafter, as we purpofe taking Salifbury in our way to town.

But to return to the profpect from White
Parifh

Parish Hill. The northern extent of it is
bounded by the plains; which gradually
join a luxurious cover that sweeps round
the eastern boundaries of the vale, and
mingles with the bolder promontories that
close the right hand view. The other side
view, which still possesses high ascents, is
well watered and wooded in its vallies;
and breaks into large sweeping curves of
the vale, through which the flowing Avon
meanders, and discharges itself at Christ
Church.

Lord Radnor's castle, from this wonderful ascent, (for wonderful it might be truly
called) is a conspicuous object. Still the
opposite plains form an amphitheatre; when
a break to the westward, introducing the
very nearest boundaries of Dorsetshire, helps
to finish the distance of this part. Wiltshire to the south-west still binds the valley;
till a small hill, rather deformed, abruptly,
but not unpleasantly, terminates the west-
ern view.

Hampshire, with all its wonted splendor,

now

now breaks from its remote receffes, and
vying with the pleafant fcenes of Wiltfhire,
burfts forth into every extravagance that
Nature can poffibly boaft. The proud plants
of the foreft difdaining their bounds, fpread
every profufion the moft verdant foliage
can poffefs; making by its grandeur fuch an
elevated impreffion on the mind, as is not
foon erazed. This delightful fcene ftill
continued through the whole extent from
weft to eaft; and as if Nature thought fhe
could not do enough to gratify the fight
upon this occafion, fhe introduced a defirable limit of the ocean, with all the picturefque beauties of the Ifle of Wight.

Having received every gratification fuch
a lovely fcene could afford, we returned towards Romfey. From this fweep of beauty
we defcended to a lane, bounded on both
fides, for three miles, by hedge rows.—The
village of White Parifh is pleafant, but there
is little worth notice to be met with at it.
The very northern extent of the foreft
croffes the road here, and produces a fcene
perfectly

perfectly different from what we had feen before.

A gravel pit gave a luftre to its fore-ground. The figures and cattle, which confifted of a few cows, and a cart loaded with the produce of the pit, were fo well adapted to the fcene, that had we chofen their difpofition, we could not have grouped them to fo much advantage as they had done themfelves. A fine broken cottage, with half of its roof covered with flate, the remainder covered with thatch overgrown with mofs, relieved the variegated ftone of which the fabric was conftructed.—A window half open,—and a door fhattered by time,—added beauty to the furze and heath that furrounded its entrance. A noble afh entwining its branches with a twifted pine, fheltered its right fide; while a ftately oak, which nearly extended its boughs to the afh, brought forward the cottage from its recefs. The only deficiency was the want of a pale diftance to give the true poetic fcope to the picture.

Little

Little of any thing interefting prefented itfelf till we had paffed the heath.. Curiofity here excited us to view a bog of fome length, lying on Sherfield-Englifh common. It commences clofe to the road, and extends over many parts of the common. We endeavoured to find its bottom, but could not fathom it with a pole of ten feet long. In order to try the firmnefs of the furface, we fent a dog that we had with us upon it; but the rains having rendered it incapable of bearing any weight, it was with difficulty the animal extricated himfelf.

On the right hand lies Milch-Wood, a pleafant feat, the refidence of colonel Ofborne, which commands a very extenfive profpect. The houfe, from the road, appears to be a well-built, convenient, and neat manfion; and the grounds are fpacious, but with very few embellifhments. A little farther on to the left, is Mr. Lockart's, a modern brick building. A fmall ftream, apparently branching from the river Beft, paffes its fides, and is the principal object that catches the eye.

As

As we afcended Dunmore hill, the magnificent afpect of the new foreft began to
grow more extenfive. The rugged heath
which we had paffed the preceeding day, now
fore-fhortened itfelf; and helped to give altitude to the chain of hills we had obferved
to join Wiltfhire.—The colouring of thefe was
fuperb.—Only the pencil of Mr. Farrington
could have done juftice to them. The fun
was bright; and flying clouds, catching
alternately at their tops, prefented excel-
lencies we have fo often feen in this mafter.

The wonderful boldnefs and majefty with
which thefe hills rofe, afforded us greater
pleafure than we had yet received. The lines
were gracefully irregular, and all that a
painter could poffibly defire.—No formal
hedge-rows appeared to difpleafe the fight;
and even the heath before mentioned, which
had appeared fo difguftful, when we were
on it, now added to the vivacity of the imagination;—the fun catching forcibly on its
barren broom, and gravelly foil, produced
a fine light to relieve the variegated diftance.
From henceforth I fhall not defpife the
                                    meaneft

meaneſt object that nature preſents ; for, if the ſubject might not happen to ſuit the immediate ſight, I am well convinced, that although for the moment in which you traverſe it, the appearance may diſguſt ; yet when ſeen in another point of view, it will anſwer ſome good purpoſe, and contribute, in ſome meaſure, towards the effect. Thus, in the view before us, the heath gave that contraſted beauty to the towering groves of the foreſt, which they could not derive from a corn field, or the bright hue of the bladed graſs ; it blending ſo charmingly with the lower parts of the wood, which gradually decreaſed its noble dimenſions as it deſcended into the winding vale.

The form and elegance ſo grand a burſt of landſcape diſplays to the ſight, makes us deſpiſe that littleneſs which nature frequently ſpreads around her other works. As I have before obſerved, every ſhrub, though highly diſguſting at the inſtant, may have charms when properly ſtudied.

From Dunmore the views are excellent,
and

and command the entire furrounding country. Dunmore is a hill, raifed in the middle of a fpacious amphitheatre, and equal to any in this county. The fea and the Ifle of Wight are no fmall objects from it. Declining its fide, we had a perfect garden at its foot. The river Beft, breaking from the left-hand hills, which contribute no inconfiderable fhare towards the harmony of the other parts, caught the frequent paffing fhadows of the flying fubftances, and heightened the tints of the flowers that decked the opening valley. While we furveyed this fcene we could not help fancying that it had given rife to the following defcription in Goldfmith's traveller.

" Lakes, forefts, cities, plains extended wide,
" The pomp of kings, the fhepherds humble pride."

Romfey church was equally picturefque, and added to the view. The north window gave a noble appearance to the venerable building ; nor was the fpire lefs obfervable, darting through the furrounding trees which hid the lower part of it. With cautious fteps we defcended the hill and took a view of the meandering

meandring vale, the beauties of which are
numberlefs; but as we cannot introduce
them fufficiently here to do them juftice, we
muft omit any defcription of them.

The town of Rumfey, or Romfey, is very
ancient, and ftill boafts of fome refpectability
from its church, which is a fine old Gothic
building. The external appearance of it is
fair, and has an air of grandeur. It is
chiefly conftructed of ftone, of fo durable a
nature, that the deftructive hand of time
feems to have made little or no impreffion on
its walls. The infide is likewife in good repair. The entrance to the chapels is very
fpacious; and there are a few curious ftatues;
but, like many other wife corporations, the
corporation of this town having raifed a fubfcription for the purpofe, they have been at
great pains to *beautify*, alias, to *obliterate* and
deface its internal appearance. The form of
the church is that of a crofs, with femicircular
chapels in the upper angles. On the top of
it grows an apple tree. Near the large
window in the fouth crofs tranfept, is a
figure of confiderable fize, in baffo relievo,

Vol. I.   H   reprefenting

reprefenting our Saviour. Sir William Petty, the fon of an eminent clothier of this town, and one of the anceftors of the prefent marquis of Landfdown, lies buried in the church, with only his name infcribed on the ftone, notwithftanding he was fo celebrated a character.

The army of Cromwell, among their wanton devaftations in this part of the kingdom, fired feveral cannon fhot againft the church, but not enough to deface it much. The impreffion of feveral are ftill vifible on the walls of the north crofs aile.

A monaftery of Benedictine nuns was founded here by king Edgar, who were afterwards removed by him to fome other part of the county. A daughter of king Stephen was an abbefs of it, but her marriage with Matthew of Alface fo incenfed the clergy, that large rewards were offered for taking her hufband, and delivering him up to the incitements of their religious zeal, whether alive or dead. So offended were thefe bigots at the lady's relinquifhing her holy

ftation

ſtation, that they pronounced her union with the prince of Alſace little ſhort of inceſt.

In the time of Henry the Third, a petition from the lady abbeſs of this convent was preſented to the king, praying that ſhe might be permitted to erect a gallows for the execution of criminals. Her application was favourably received, and letters patent for that purpoſe were not only granted her, but alſo a juriſdiction for trying them.

A large manufactory for ſhalloons was formerly carried on in this town; but the cheapneſs of labour in the northern parts of the kingdom, with the conſequent ſuperiority of the goods made there, has of late years cauſed a very conſiderable decreaſe in that branch.

According to the opinion of Dr. Stukely, this town was a Roman ſtation, to which they gave the name of Arminis. Lord Palmerſton's ſeat, already deſcribed, lies a little to left of it.

Having

Having a wish to take a view of the scenes which present themselves on the road to Hursley, we left the near way to Southampton, and took the left hand road. The views we had in the morning, now appeared less grand; which was occasioned by our being below the level of the general sight at that time. A few straggling cottages at the entrance of sir William Heathcote's woods have every beauty a woody entrance usually produces. It continues a perfect grove for near three miles; and we may point it out as a pleasant ride from Southampton. Thatchbury Mount has to boast of having been the residence of kings. It is now the property of the Heathcote family.

The evening advancing apace, the declining sun gave additional beauty to the surrounding woods. A purple tint diffused itself in the distance that verged into the water of Hampton, and exhibited fresh proofs of the picturesque appearance of Hampshire. Crossing Cranbury Common, we arrived, about twilight, at Hampton, after a pleasant tour of three days.

SECTION

SECTION V.

BISHOP's Waltham being the place we
intended to vifit next, we left Southampton before day-break, in order to fee
the effect produced by the rifing of the fun.
By the time our horfes had croffed Itching
ferry, we obferved a light burfting through
a cloud on the downs; we therefore haftened
to Pear-tree Green ; but to our great difappointment, the mift inftantaneoufly vanifh-
ing, the fun broke up. We had pleafed ourfelves with the hopes of beholding a ftrong
expellant from the fun, owing to a thick
mift that had fpread itfelf upon the water;
the great power of that orb, in the month
of Auguft, was, however, not adapted to the
occafion.

The heath, enlivened by the pearly dew,
fpangling with morning webs the furface of
the whithered fern, fhone in a multiplicity
of colours, and had fufficient attraction for
the fight, as well as for the improvement of

colouring

colouring a morning fore-ground. The oppofite fhores of Fawley now fhone forth
with all their attractions. A fine harmo-
nizing glare of pale yellow ftreaked along
the oak-bound ftrand, that juft verged upon
the fhore, and imperceptibly crept into the
ftronger tints of the green and blue by which
the river's furface was ftained. Hamble river,
and its banks, lay beneath the fhadow of the
adjacent hills.

Inclining to the left, we croffed into the
road near Botley. This town ftands on a hill,
and among its inhabitants has feveral genteel families. The buildings are chiefly brick
and plafter. At the lower end of the town
are feveral mills, the beft in the county for
convenience and capacioufnefs.

Here we quitted the high road, and ftruck
over the downs which lie to the left, where
frefh fcenes at every inftant encountered the
fight. The diftant parts of the county joining the hills of Suffex, appeared fo beautifully diverfified with wood, water, and mountains, that it brought another part of Gold-
smith's

fmith's picturefque " Traveller" to our re-
collection :

> " Her uplands floping, deck the mountain's fide,
> " Woods over woods in gay theatric pride ;
> " While oft fome temple's mouldering top between,
> " With venerable grandeur marks the fcene."

A range of woods declining from the fight,
rufhed down the mountain's fide to tafte the
rivers flow, and join the bending poplar's
nod, that overhung the beachy clift, and,
unconfcious of their charms, in fweet confufion, fpread along the bafis of the mountains, to eafe the line of many a rugged ftep.
Such fcenes frequently encounter the eye
near Botley, and afford inconceivable pleafure to the enraptured mind.

Botley common leads to the lower parts of
Wykeham foreft, the trees of which are
high, and chiefly oak, with very little un-
derwood; a circumftance that renders the
gentlemens' feats in thefe parts well fituated
for hunting.

During our excurfions in the New Foreft
we had frequently obferved the cattle about

noon

noon to affociate together in herds. Here we had an opportunity of feeing great numbers of them collected together on the top of a hill, and we found that it was cuftomary for cows and horfes to affemble in a body, in order to fcreen each other from the fcorching beams of the fun during the midday heat. They ufually chufe for that purpofe fome elevated place, that they might enjoy the refrefhing breeze; and are obferved every day to frequent nearly the fame fpot. In one place to which we reforted for feveral fucceffive days, we particularly remarked that we always found the fame heifers, colts, and other cattle, we had feen there the preceding day; and that, not ten yards diftant from the fpot, nor ten minutes fooner or later. In the evenings we as furely found them cheft-high in the fame water, in the adjacent valley. Nor is it unufual for them, when they are overburthened with flies, to run full fpeed to the water, plunge themfelves in, and lie on their fides till they have difengaged themfelves from their tormenting companions.

From

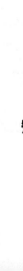

From the Foreſt of Wykeham, we made
for Biſhop's Waltham, or as it is termed by
the country people, the Biſhop's Abbey.
The remains of this abbey plainly evince
that it was once a place of ſome conſequence. One tower only at preſent remains, and that is in a ſhattered condition.
The building, however, though much defaced by time, is in its higheſt ſtate of perfection for the canvas. The walls are overgrown with ivy ; which, notwithſtanding it
had contributed to reduce the fabric to its
preſent ruinous ſtate, now lends its utmoſt
aid to prevent its mouldering ſides from ſink-
ing into oblivion.

The inſide of the priory is appropriated
to the uſes of a farm yard ; and ſuch parts
of the walls as remain, are covered in, and
become barns and cart-hovels. The town
of Biſhop's Waltham is a ſmall, diſagreeable, ill-paved, inconvenient ſpot, and poſſeſſed of no one requiſite to make it other-
wiſe. It received the name of Biſhop's Waltham, from its being formerly a palace of
the biſhop of Wincheſter.

Some

Some years ago a party of the inhabitants of this town retired to a recluse dell in the foreſt, from whence they iſſued forth during the night; and, their numbers rendering them formidable, committed depredations in the neighbourhood, killing deer, ſheep, &c. for their ſubſiſtence. As they chiefly made their appearance in the night, they were named the *Waltham Blacks*. The place of their reſidence was a receſs, inacceſſible by any other way than a ſubterraneous paſſage. They dreſſed like foreſters; the croſs-bow was their weapon; and ſome ſay they aſſerted that they were the deſcendants of Robin Hood; certain however it is, that they lived, like him, by plunder. In this licentious ſtate they remained a conſiderable time; and at laſt were diſperſed by the activity of the neighbouring gentlemen.

We left Biſhop's Waltham without regret, and croſſed the foreſt to Wykeham; which, whether it be denominated a village or a town, ſtands on a pleaſant, healthy ſpot. It has ſeveral good houſes in it, and is a poſt town on the road to Goſport, from which

it

it is diftant nine miles; from Portfmouth fourteen. Little elfe is recorded of it, befides its having had the honour of being the birth-place of William of Wykeham.

This celebrated perfon, whofe parents were people of mean rank in the town of Wyke-ham, received his education at Weftminfter fchool, and by his great abilities made his way to the higheft offices. Edward the Third finding him a fkilful architect, ap-pointed him furveyor of the royal buildings, with a handfome allowance. Windfor caf-ftle, the favourite refidence of that king, was built under his infpection; and having exe-cuted many other works with equal judg-ment and fidelity, he was rewarded by his majefty with feveral high preferments both civil and ecclefiaftical, till at length he fuc-ceeded to the fee of Winchefter, and was appointed lord high chancellor. His me-mory has been immortalized by the noble foundations which owe their exiftence to him. Among the chief of thefe are his college at Winchefter, and New College at Oxford. The cathedral of Winchefter, as

before

before obferved, was rebuilt by him in its
prefent magnificent ftile, and he lies interred therein. He died at his palace in
Bifhop's Waltham.

As, in order the better to purfue the purpofe of our journey, we never travelled in
a public road, but when it was not poffible
to take any other, we now ftruck into the
private one leading over the heath to Southwick. Near the road's fide ftands the houfe
of Mr. Garnier, pleafantly laid out with a
park and gardens. Here we particularly
kept the right hand, which led through a
village, and fkirted the wood-fide. Nothing
remarkable prefented itfelf but that of its
being a bad ftony road, and in fome parts
nearly up to the horfes' knees in fand. By
the fide of it, a large track of boggy common land, continued for a very confiderable
diftance, which hurt the eye. This rocky
road lafted moft of our way to Southwick.

At the entrance of this town is a fmall
rivulet, which rufhing over a few pebbles,
relieves the oppofite cottages. At the entrance

trance of the town were feveral brick houfes,
the appearance of which was ungrateful to
the fight, and the more fo as they precluded
the greater beauties of the broken fides of
many a mouldering hut.

Mr. Thiftlewaite has a large houfe on
the left hand at the bottom of the town,
which appears quite deferted. The grounds
around it are fpacious, but they are in bad
order.

SECTION

SECTION VI.

THE whole of the road from Southwick to Ports-down hill, which was now the fpot to which we bent our courfe, is compofed of flint ftones, by which our horfes' legs were much cut. The fun being on the decline, we made all the fpeed we could to reach that place, in order to enjoy, by his declining rays, the beautiful profpects it is well known to afford. The foil of the hill confifts of a chalky furface, with a bed of flint underneath; and where cultivated is very productive.

Nor were we difappointed in our expectations, when we had reached the fummit, which was about half an hour before the fun fet. The views were indeed noble and extenfive beyond defcription. The firft fcenes that prefented themfelves to the eaftward were Suffex hills. The fpire of Chichefter cathedral caught the full force of the fun's rays, and fhone in every fplendor wherewith the Smiths' of that town have

pourtrayed

pourtrayed it. The ridge of mountains
which feparate Petworth from the fea, though
thirty miles diftant, were perfectly vifible;
and through a part where the chain was
abruptly broken, the hill of Petworth peep-
ed up to foften the diftance.

The hills of Hampfhire again proved a
foil to their neighbours, and launching their
foliage along their verdant brows, funk by
degrees into the valley of Southwick. The
fpire of that village, encircled by the trees,
was pleafing to the eye. Hambleton hills
to the north-weft were agreeable, but not
fo bold as thofe of Suffex. Here the valley
again encountered the fight, and uniting
feveral fmall purling ftreams into one body,
added frefh luftre to the dale.

To paint with true colouring and juftice
the hills which range towards Wiltfhire, is
beyond the reach of my pen. The magnificence with which each reared its head, and
leaned upon its neighbour's brow, with here
and there an irregular picturefque broken
mountain, juft rifing its woody promontory

to

... not ... the ... well view.

... the hill ... to the extensive ... below. It was one of ... what the lowering ... its circumference, ... to all its rays ... glide to the ... with its fire, ... in the evening.—A moment when

to skirt along its foot, and blend it with the valley, gave grace and sublimity to the scene. The Wiltshire plains rather evenly, but not unpleasantly, appeared on fire from the reflection of the sun, and closed the north-west view.

The woods of Hampshire now resumed their former lustre, and stretching round to the south-west, brought the noble mountains we see at Dunmore, to a termination at Lymington. Dorsetshire swept along our horizon, (which the elevation of the spot we were on rendered uncommonly extensive) and introduced the Isle of Portland into the distance. All the forest of Hampshire was clothed in its wonted splendor. The sun, now gradually declining the hill, launched its glorious hues to the extensive fertile valley that lay below. It was one of those picturesque sun-sets, when the hovering clouds gather round its circumference, and only permit it partially to cast its rays on some flowery vale, and glide up the mountain's side, dazzling with its lustre, and striking with its colouring.—A moment

when

... the ... ...
... ...
... ... not
... ... appe... ... ... the
... ... before, ...
of view.

The ... ...
... ...
... ...
... ...
... ... our
... ... the elev...on of the spot
... ...
... ... of ... land
... ...
... ... of grandeur.
... now ... ...ing the hill,
... ... over to the extensive
... ... than below. In ... ... of
... ... sets, when the lover-
... ... its circumference,
d... ... ... y to mix its rays
... ... globe in the
... ... with ... fire,
... ... will ... ...—A. ... ment
                                              when

when the mind of the contemplative obferver muft be impreffed with the moft pleafing fenfations.

The Ifle of Wight, with its floping hills
and ouzy fhore, is feen from Ports-down to
every advantage; the eye at once taking in
the eaftern part St. Helen's, and its weftern-
moft point, the Needles. From this fpot
Portfmouth harbour likewife receives every
addition its inceffant turns can give it.

The Caftle of Porchefter was in our fore-
ground. This building is faid to have been
erected by Gurgentius, one of the Britifh
kings, before the commencement of the Chriftian æra. According to tradition, the village
of Porchefter is the place where Vefpafian the
Roman emperor landed when he came to
Britain. Here was anciently a large harbour, for the defence of which the caftle
was built; but the fea gradually retiring
from it, till there was not a fufficient depth
of water for veffels of burthen, the inhabitants removed to Portfea. Henry the Firft
founded here a priory of Auguftine canons,

which appears to have been foon after removed to Southwick; where it continued
till the diffolution, when it was valued at
two hundred and fifty-feven pounds four
fhillings and four-pence a year. Two of
the towers of the caftle are ftill ftanding.
The court-yard is fpacious, and contains a
chapel. The whole is furrounded by a wall,
very perfect, with battlements on the top;
but the infide is much injured by time, and
mouldering faft to decay. It commands an
uninterrupted view of Portfmouth harbour,
and of the furrounding country. The principal ufe it has been put to of late years,
has been that of a place of confinement for
the French prifoners during a war.

The men of war lying at Spithead appear
from Ports-down Hill like fmall fpots on the
water. The fouth-eaft point of Portfea
ftretches to Thorly Ifland, where it retires
to the Suffex coaft. The blue curtain of
night, now foftly lowered on the mountain's brow, delightfully harmonized the
aërial fubftances with the mifty dales, and
clofed our evening fcenes.

Defcending

Defcending the hill, we entered the out-
works of Portfmouth; and paffed feveral
drawbridges, with many improvements
made in the fortifications of that place by
direction of his grace the duke of Richmond;
but the evening being clofed in, we muft
have loft the fight of many interefting fubjects in the military line, that lay in our way
to the town.

At this place the emprefs Maud landed,
when fhe came to difpute the right of king
Stephen to the crown of England.

Portfmouth received its name from its fituation at the mouth of an æftuary, which
at high water furrounds a tract of country
about fourteen miles in circumference, called Portfea Ifland. Its fortifications were
begun by Edward the Fourth, and augmented by Henry the Seventh, and his fon
Harry the Eighth; they were afterwards
greatly improved by queen Elizabeth; but
to Charles the Second do they chiefly owe
their prefent ftrength, extent, and magnificence. That Portfmouth is a place of fome

antiquity,

antiquity, might be proved from an hofpital called God's Houfe, dedicated to John the Baptift, and Saint Nicholas, which was founded here by Peter de Rupibus, and at the diffolution was valued at thirty-three pounds nineteen fhillings and five-pence per annum.

The Common is now the moft confiderable part of Portfmouth; but nothing more than the chapel of St. John, and the dock-yard, are worth infpection. The former is a beautiful modern building, ornamented in the infide with pillars of the Ionic order. We regretted that the architect was not known to us. The organ, by England, is a fine piece of mechanifm, and much admired both for its tone and appearance.

The dockyard, I need not fay, is allowed to be the completeft, probably, in the world. A great number of labourers of every kind are employed in it. The warehoufes, containing the ftores, are numerous and fpacious; and all the buildings remarkably clean and neat. Commiffioner Martin refides in a
handfome

handfome houfe within the walls of the yard, which are at leaft two miles in circumference; and through the vigilance and indefatigable attention of that gentleman, every care is taken to fecure this invaluable arfenal at once from the infpéction of foreigners, and the attempts of ill-difpofed perfons.

The fortifications have of late been greatly improved and augmented by the prefent mafter-general of the ordnance, his grace of Richmond. The entrance of the harbour is defended on the eaft by Southfea Caftle, and towards the weft by Monckton Fort, fituated oppofite the Mother Bank. The former was eré́cted by king Henry the Eighth, was of great ftrength, and lies about a mile and a half fouth of the town. On the land-fide the town is ftrongly fortified by works of confiderable extent.

Portfmouth was incorporated by king Charles the Firft, and is governed by a mayor, aldermen, recorder, and common-

council.

council. A fair is held here on the sixteenth
of July, which lasts fourteen days.

Gosport, situated on the opposite side of
the harbour, is a place well known, and
much reforted to by perfons in the maritime
line, but elfe of little note. Veffels fail at
ftated periods from hence to Guernfey, Jerfey, and the adjacent iflands. A hoy goes
from hence to Southampton three times a
week, and one to Cowes every day. But the
packet-boats for the foregoing iflands, and
for Cowes, fail from Southampton.

The harbour of Portfmouth has a fine
bottom, with from three to nine fathom
water. There are feveral channels in it
which are navigable at high water as far up
as Fareham, a town about feven miles diftant,
and which makes a pleafant aquatic excurfion. As we went up, we left Porchefter
Caftle to the right ;—the hills of Ports-down
clofed the view. Thefe hills, though rather
too formal in their lines to give pleafure, yet
ferve to relieve the near diftances. Fareham
is

is a healthy little fifhing town; but as we only ftaid there while we took fome refrefh-ment, we had no opportunity of making any enquiries relative to it. We returned to Portfmouth by a different channel than that by which we had gone.

From Porchefter Caftle, the entrance of the harbour has an excellent appearance. Spithead, with the fhips at anchor there, are confpicuous objects ;—the Ifle of Wight the diftance.—As it would be impoffible, without fwelling the work too much, to en-ter into a particular defcription of this place, with its immenfe piles of fortifications and buildings, we have only given the foregoing curfory fketch of it.

Having fhipped our horfes, we now em-barked for the ifland which had been the primary object of our Tour.—Cowes was the place of our deftination.—As we paffed Monkton Fort, we could not help taking notice of the number of new works which were erecting, and which muft greatly tend to the fecurity of this important place.

We

We had fcarcely paffed the fort before
the heavens frowned, and a violent ftorm
threatened us; but inftead of being appre-
henfive of the confequences, we awaited the
expected combuftion of the elements with a
pleafing impatience, that we might obferve
the grand effect it muft produce.—A hail-
ftorm was the forerunner.—The fea, though
fo near the fhore, rolled in with a heavy
fwell;—and the waves, cafting their light
foam on the furface of the ebbing tide, were
caught by the rays of the fetting fun, which
darted through a cloud; while feveral tranfits of light from the fame fource tinged the
flowing fails of the numerous barks, that,
under different tacks, fkimmed along the
furrounding ocean. The wind at length
abating, the fwell alfo in fome degree fub-
fided; and we were again able to keep the
deck. The remaining part of the evening
proved clear and agreeable; but at the time
the evening gun was fired at Portfmouth,
we were ftill four miles diftant from the
harbour of Cowes. At this diftance the
fhores appeared to be covered with every
luxuriance the richeft foil can boaft.—The
ftorm

ſtorm had been ſucceeded by a calm; at length however a favourable breeze ſpringing up, we reached Cowes Road about ten o'clock, after a tedious paſſage of ſeven hours.

SECTION

SECTION VII.

BEFORE we proceed to give a particular account of the places we vifited on this ifland, and the picturefque fcenes that prefented themfelves, a general, but concife, defcription of it may not prove unacceptable to our readers.

The Ifle of Wight was a part of the territories anciently inhabited by the Belgæ, and was brought under fubjection to the Romans during the reign of the emperor Claudian. By them it was called Vecta, or Vectis. It was afterwards conquered by Cerdic, king of the Weft Saxons, who peopled it with Jutes, a tribe that had accompanied the Saxons into England. Cadwaller, a fucceeding king of the Weft Saxons, is faid to have made himfelf mafter of it fome time after, and to have maffacred moft of the inhabitants. Having undergone many other revolutions and invafions, it at length, together with the iflands of Jerfey and Guernfey, was erected into a kingdom by king Henry
the

the Sixth, and beftowed on Henry de Beau-
champ, duke of Warwick, whom he crowned
the fovereign of it with his own hands; but
the duke dying without iffue, thefe iflands
loft their royalty, and again reverted to the
crown.

It is fituated oppofite to the coaft of
Hampfhire, from which it is divided by a
channel, varying in breadth from two to
feven miles. It conftitutes a part of the
county of Southampton, and is within the
diocefe of Winchefter. Its greateft length,
extending from eaft to weft, is more than
twenty miles; its breadth, from north to
fouth, about thirteen; and above feventy
miles in circumference. The form of it is
fomewhat of an irregular oval. Newport,
the capital town, which is feated nearly in
the centre of the ifland, is upwards of
eighty miles diftant from London.

The air in general is healthy, and the foil
fertile. The north part affords excellent
pafturage and meadow grounds, while the
fouth is a fine corn country. A great number

ber of fheep are likewife fed upon a ridge of mountains running through the middle of the ifland. Their wool, which is remarkable for its finenefs, is a valuable article of trade to the inhabitants. Among the natural productions of this ifland, is the milk-white tobacco-pipe clay, of which large quantities are exported, and likewife a fine white fand, of which drinking-glaffes, &c. are made. A more particular account of thefe will be given when we fpeak of the places where they are found,

Such is the purity of the air, the fertility of the foil, and the beauty and variety of its landfcapes, that it has been often ftiled *The Garden of England*. Parties of pleafure are on that account frequently made to it; but thefe excurfions are generally confined to Carifbrooke Caftle, the Needles, and a few other places; while it abounds with delightful fcenes which recommend it to the attention of the artift. Of the principal of thefe we fhall endeavour in the fubfequent pages to give our readers fome idea.

The

The craggy cliffs and rocks by which this ifland is encircled, form a natural fortification, particularly on the fouth-fide. Sandown fort defends the only part which is left by Nature open to the invafion of an enemy.

It is divided into two hundreds, feparated by the river Medham or Medina, which gives name to them ; they being called, according to their fituation with refpect to that river, Eaft and Weft Medina. Thefe hundreds contain three market towns, fifty-two parifhes, and about twenty thoufand inhabitants.

The morning after we had landed at Cowes, was not lefs beautiful than the preceding evening had been interefting. The firft object which attracted our attention on the ifland, was Cowes Caftle. It is a fmall ftone building, with a femicircular battery, fituated on the weft-fide of the river Medina. Oppofite to it, on the eaft-fide of the river was formerly another fort of the fame kind ; and, when entire, they jointly protected the harbour ;

bour; but the latter is now so totally demolished, that there is not the least vestige of it remaining. The castle at West Cowes was erected by Henry the Eighth; it is a plain building, with a platform before it, on which are mounted a few cannon. The works have lately been repaired by order of his grace the duke of Richmond.

The best view of it is on the decline of the beach towards the bathing machines. Here the castle assumes another form, and shows the round tower with the distant battlement. A group of trees close the view in one point;—the opening of the opposite shore, among the trees, is agreeable and striking.

The town of West Cowes stands on a rising ground, at the mouth of the river Medina. Its appearance, when near it, much resembles Gravesend water-side; but the internal part is far more pleasant and commodious;—the streets however are narrow, and the town upon the whole indifferently built.

Cowes

Cowes owes its origin and increafe to its
excellent harbour ; where fhips are not only
fecure from ftorms, but fo happily fituated,
as to be able to turn out either to the eaftward or weftward, every tide. It is well
peopled, and enjoys a good trade for the fale
of provifions, efpecially in time of war, when
large fleets of merchant fhips often ride
here for feveral weeks, waiting either for a
wind or convoy. The inhabitants are in
general genteel and polite, without being
troublefomely ceremonious. Many gentlemen belonging to the navy, have feats adjoining to this town, amongft which are
thofe of captain Chriftian and captain Bafk-
erville. Mr. White has one here, and another on the banks of the Medina, called
Fairlee.

Eaft Cowes, which lies on the oppofite
point of land, has very defirable beauties
with regard to its appearance and fituation,
together with convenience for families, that
is not exceeded at Weft Cowes ; but it has
not the fame advantages with refpect to
bathing.

The

The fare from Cowes to Portfmouth and Southampton, as well for paffengers as for their horfes, carriages, &c. is fettled by the corporation of Newport; by which means impofitions, that might otherwife occur, are prevented.

The market is well fupplied with fifh from Torbay, and Southampton river; the former has the fuperiority for turbot, the latter for foles. Upon the whole, the accommodations at Cowes are equal to thofe of any other watering place, and much more reafonable. The town is enlarging, and from its pleafant vicinities attracts every year an increafe of company.

From Mr. Lynn's cottage, at the top of the hill, a very extenfive view fweeps the diftance. Cowes lies in a bird's eye view, with the full profpect of the veffels in its road, and the oppofite woody point. The hills of Ports-down are very diftinctly feen; but from their remotenefs, and the large body of water that lies between, we had not (except at times, when the ruffling wind caught in fudden
den

den patches on the water's furface) a fufficient interefting fcene to defcribe, farther than
as to its extenfivenefs.

The evening being clear, we fet off for
Newport. The road from Cowes to that
place is equal in goodnefs to any in England.
A hedged row hemmed us in on both fides,
and prevented us from enjoying the profpects that furrounded us. A houfe at the
extremity of Cowes, received its name of
Birmingham, as the neighbours report, from
the poffeffor of it paying his men with coun-
terfeit half-pence.

On the road lies the village of Northwood,
and to the left of it is Midham, the feat of
Mr. Green.

The Foreft of Alvington, King's Foreft,
or Parkhurft, by which names it is feverally
called, opens very picturefquely;—a bold
range of hills, with St. Catherine for its
crown, binds the diftance. The lines of the
hills are charmingly irregular, and blend
into each other's fweeps.

On the left hand, the curve of the river takes an opening, and ſhines with reflections of the neighbouring ſhores. To the right, the grandeur of the hills gradually dimi-niſhes, and they are at length obſcured by the promontories of the foreſt.

The general hoſpital of the iſland ſtands adjoining to the road, about half a mile be-fore you reach Newport, where thoſe who unfortunately are obliged to court the um-brage of its charitable walls, are treated with great humanity and attention.

The entrance to Newport is ſuch as we generally find when a river meanders near it. A bridge is the principal objeçt ; but this is too contemptible in its appearance for a picture. Its uſual companion, the buſy mill, lies on the right hand of it. At St. Croſs, on the left, is the ſeat of Mr. Kirkpatrick.

The town of Newport is perhaps the pleaſanteſt in this part of the kingdom. The houſes are plain and neat ; the ſtreets uni-form ; and, except at the weſt end, all regularly

larly paved. The church is alfo a eonfpicu-
ous and leading feature to its neatnefs ; but
it is fomewhat remarkable, that though belonging to fo populous a place, it is only a
chapel of eafe annexed to the little village of
Carifbrook.

Here are two affembly rooms, and a neat
theatre, lately erected ; together with a free
grammar fchool which was built by public
fubfcription ; the fchool-room is fifty feet
long, with convenient accommodations for
the mafter.

Two markets are held here every week,
in which great quantities of all forts of grain
and provifions are difpofed of, not only for
the ufe of the inhabitants, but for fupplying
the outward bound fhips, many of which,
as before obferved, touch at Cowes. When
I mention the market, I muft not forget to
notice alfo the farmers' daughters who refort to it with the produce of their farms,
and at once grace it with the charms of their
perfons, and the winning affability of their
behaviour. There is not perhaps in the

kingdom

kingdom a place where fo many lovely girls attend the market as at Newport ; and, at the fame time they are dreffed with a degree of elegance far beyond what is ufually obfervable in perfons of their rank. You fee them, with health and fprightlinefs in their looks, lightly difmount from their forefters, and conveying their bafkets, each to her chair, tender their butter, eggs, and fowls to fale, with a graceful eafe and complaifance, without making ufe of thofe arts that are generally practifed to procure cuftomers, or ever abating of the price they afk. On the two principal market days held here, viz. at Whitfuntide and Michaelmas, it is not uncommon to fee thirty or forty of them all dreffed in fo genteel a ftile, and behaving with fo much unaffected complaifance and dignity, that a ftranger might be eafily led to take them for perfons of quality *en mafquerade*. The appearance of thefe charming girls not only excited our wonder and admiration, but we found that they attracted the envy of all the farmers' daughters on the neighbouring coafts. The market houfe is in the middle of the town ; and

they

they have alfo a new market appropriated
to the fale of corn.

The town of Newport is fituated fo nearly
in the centre of the ifland, (the exact centri-
cal fpot lying not a mile to the fouthward of
it,) that it is thereby rendered alike convenient to the inhabitants of every part. We
could not acquire a minute account of the
number of perfons of both fexes refident in
it, but the houfes are fuppofed to amount to
near fix hundred;—they are chiefly conftructed of brick, and in general are not
lofty.

Newport was incorporated by James the
Firft, and is governed by a mayor, recorder,
and twelve aldermen; who, I might fay
without flattery, are much more deferving
the title of *gentlemen*, than fome who have
paffed under our infpection fince the commencement of our Tour.

Few places afford better accommodations
for genteel people, who may vifit this ifland,
either on parties of pleafure, or for the

K 3

benefit

benefit of their health, than Newport. The defire of giving fatisfaction feems to be the predominant feature of thofe who keep the principal inns; and by their civility and conveniencies, they have of late years attracted much company.

SECTION

SECTION VIII.

AS we purpofed keeping the coaft from Newtown, we croffed the country to that place. In our way we entered the foreft of Alvington, and purfuing a tract (high road there was none) that inclined to the north-weft, at length ftruck into a ftony lane, where we had an excellent view of Carifbrook hills; whofe mountainous appearance was relieved by a woody valley, that gently floping from the foreft brow, gradually dwindled into the dale.

Still purfuing our courfe through the ftony lane, we paffed a copfe of oaks, where the mountains juft mentioned received every flafh of grandeur the folar rays could produce. The fea, on the right, now opened gradually, and afforded us tranfitory views of the mouth of Southampton river, of Lutterel's Folly, the entrance of Beaulieu river, St. Leonard's, and likewife of Lymington creek.

K 4

As

As we afcended thefe northern eminences, we had a view fufficiently extenfive to perceive that a range of hills, or rather mountains, runs through the centre of the ifland. I think I may with fome degree of exactnefs fix their commencement at Carifbrook Caftle, as a valley opens between them, that takes a direct courfe from the moft northern extremity, Cowes, to the foot of St. Catherine's.

Thefe mountains fweep to the fouth-weft, and terminate their range a little beyond Calborne. Here another dale feparates them from Afton downs, and the Yarmouth hills, which decline rather more to the weftward. Frefhwater-gate and Allum-bay may be clearly difcerned throughout the whole way, after you have paffed the foreft.

Alvington foreft is almoft entirely void of what generally gives the denomination of a foreft to a tract of land ; except a few pollard oaks, no trees of any confequence are to be feen upon it, till you fkirt its borders ; there indeed the oak luxuriantly intermixes with the afh and elm.

At

At the entrance of Newtown we met with one of thofe fubjects fo often touched by the pencil of Mr. Gainfborough; a cottage overfhadowed with trees; while a glimmering light, juft breaking through the branches, caught one corner of the ftone and flint fabric, and forcibly expreffed the conception of that great mafter. A few faggots, with a cart under a fhed, formed the fhadow part of the fore-ground; and the New Foreft, rearing its leafy tenants above the proudly fwelling waves, clofed the diftance.

From its name, we expected to have found Newtown, a town, or at leaft a large village; but were quite aftonifhed when we faw that it confifted only of fix or feven houfes. Many circumftances, however, tend to fupport the conjecture, that it was once a place of much greater confideration. In the reign of king Richard the Second, it was burnt by the French, and foon after rebuilt.

Newtown-bay, or as it is fometimes named, Shalfleet-lake, makes its entrance about

half

half a mile below the houfes ; but its opening wants the general accompaniments, wood
and rock, to render it grand.—The banks
are infipid, being devoid even of fufficient
boldnefs.—The point meanly fhrinks into
the fea, without a fhrub to court its ftony
flatnefs. From the frequent breaks that
open though the wood, Hampfhire was perfectly picturefque ;—the fea, as a body,
added frefh glows to the colouring, and
pleafingly varied the landfcape.

The corporation of Newtown, (for fmall
as it is, this place has to boaft a corporation,
confifting of a mayor and twelve burgeffes,
and fends two members to parliament,) an-
nually meet at the town-hall in order to
chufe the magiftrates for the year enfuing.
The manfion in which this meeting is held
has more to boaft from its fituation, than
from its elegance as a building. The only
things in it worthy of note for their antiquity are the mayoralty chair and table. The
building is of ftone, and contains three rooms,
with a cellar and kitchen underneath. A flight
of fteps lead to the council-chamber, or hall.

Shalfleet-

Shalfleet-lake falls in agreeably at the foot
of the hill; while the village and wood rife
to the left, with the downs of Brixton in its
diftance. Saltern, and Hamfted-point, relieve the Frefh-water cliffs, and bind its land
view to the eaftward.—Here thofe who tra-
vel for pleafure fhould purfue the woody
tract to the village of Shalfleet, where they
will find at every avenue frefh beauties man-
tling to the view. A body of water is preferved by dams at the foot of the town, where
a mill, entangled in the branches of its
woody fides, is an agreeable object for the
fore-ground.

On the fide of a hill, well covered with
trees, ftands the town of Shalfleet. Little
to excite curiofity is to be feen here except
the church, which from fome antiquity a-
bout it, appears to have been in the Gothic
ftile; but, like many of the churches in this
ifland, it has been robbed of its antique windows, which gave an air of grandeur and fo-
lemnity to it, and *beautified* (as they term it)
with modern cafements. We have before
cenfured this mode of beautification, and by
this

this fresh inftance are prompted to remark,
that all thofe who view with pleafure the
relics of Saxon and Gothic architecture ftill
extant, muft behold with difguft the aukward attempts of thefe good people to correct what Time has brought to that ftate of
perfection moft pleafing to the eye of a perfon of true tafte.

Nothing further worthy of attention de-
taining us, we again made for the Yarmouth
road; which having croffed, and left to the
right, we bent our courfe towards Ham-
fted-woods. The gates we had to pafs, as
the roads chiefly lie through the farmers'
grounds, were almoft innumerable; and the
foil principally confifting of clay and marle,
in fome places the roads were extremely bad.
The land, however, is very productive, and
is cultivated to the road's fide.

The principal part of the land about
Newtown, and extending to the fpot we were
travelling through, is the eftate, as we were
informed, of fir Richard Worfley. It is not
deficient towards the north-weft in woody
fceens,

ſcenes, but theſe are too thinly ſcattered to fur-
niſh a proper ſubject for a painter. The elms
range too regularly to pleaſe, and the clumps
are too formal to combine. Nor is the ſtiff
appearance of the near hedge-rows, which
encircle the corn fields, by any means grateful to the ſight ; on the contrary, ſo cloſely
placed, they are highly diſguſting. When it
is poſſible to bring them properly into the
focus of the eye, on the decline of a hill, or
on a gentle riſe, where they may blend into
each other, then indeed they give peculiar
pleaſure.

From Hamſted we had the oppoſite view
of Newtown ; but ſo encompaſſed with trees,
that little of the buildings were to be diſ-
cerned. We had however a perfect view of
Gurnet Point to the north-eaſt ; and of the
town of Yarmouth, as well as of Hurſt Caſtle
oppoſite to it, on the ſouth-weſt ; while
Lymington to the north-weſt perfected the
picture.

From Hamſted we once more returned to
the Yarmouth road, and entered it at Linwood

wood Green. Mr. Barrington's feat to the left, with its furrounding woods, are in fine order; and gracefully fill the left-hand fcene.—At the entrance of the common we obtained the nobleft view the ifland had as yet prefented us. Had not the fea towards the Ifle of Portland caufed fo large an opening, it had every appearance of a Weftmoreland fcene. The hills rofe with all the majefty of the Skiddow mountains; the valley produced a lake, with a lonely copfe to eafe its winding fhores; while the downs of Afton falling to the more ftately fweep of Frefhwater cliffs, clofe their boldnefs behind Frefhwater church. Nor were the Carifbrook hills lefs diftinguifhable; their irregular pile bringing in a proportion to the effect.

The valley was crouded with its ufual inhabitants, various kinds of cattle, and launched into every extreme the voluptuous hand of Nature could beftow; the foliage of the fore-ground harmonioufly difplayed its glowing verdure, and enchanted the fight. Every hill brought its foot to the dale, and formed a frefh avenue for the winding ftream.—The
fpire

The valley was crowded with its whole inhabitants... filled... every street... the whole army arrived of ... below; the...

... the Caribbean Islands...

spire of Freshwater, darting forth from its
vernal attendants, caught the roving eye,
and gave additional charms to the distance.
Nature here seemed yet to be in embryo, and
scarcely to have begun, what, in a few years,
will exite in the mind of every sentimental
beholder the highest pleasure and admiration. The scene behind it was not equally
inviting: the point of land between Yarmouth town and Hamsted head broke up
in the middle of it, and separated the mountains from the shores of the sea. Here Southampton water just crept in between the dis-
tances, and brought its woody range to the
surface of the river. Yarmouth, which lay
before us, did not appear so interesting as it
ought to have done, from its lying quite flat
in the point of view from which we saw it.

When we entered the town, we were not a
little disappointed, but it was an agreeable
disappointment. From its appearance at a
distance, we expected to have seen a contemptible place ; but, on the contrary, we
found the buildings in general neat and
clean, though rather low. They were mostly
                                        of

of ſtone, or whitewaſhed. If Yarmouth was paved, it would be little inferior to Newport in neatneſs.

Having often heard of Yarmouth caſtle, we went to ſee it; but how unlike a fortreſs! Scarcely any thing of ſtrength appeared about it, and as little worthy of obſervation. The view from it was the only ſatisfaction we obtained by our viſit, and that was far inferior to many ſcenes we had paſſed before.

The conveniencies of Yarmouth are very great, both to its own inhabitants, and to thoſe of the oppoſite ſhores. A paſſage-boat paſſes to and from Lymington every day, with accommodations both for paſſengers and horſes. And the paſſage from one ſhore to the other being but from five to ſix miles acroſs, it is thereby rendered reciprocally convenient to thoſe who reſide on the weſtern parts of the iſland, and to the inhabitants of the lower parts of Hampſhire and Dorſetſhire.

The ſhores abound with a great variety of ſhells, which are not found in ſuch quantities

at

at any other part of the ifland. The fifh on this coaft are chiefly foles and other flat fifh; and they are caught in fuch plenty, that they contribute greatly towards the fupport of the poor.

The borough of Yarmouth fends two members to parliament, and ranks as the third town in the ifland. It is likewife a corporate town, to which confequence it was raifed by king James the Firft. The charter directs, that when a mayor is to be elected, the inqueft by whom he is to be chofen, confifting of ten common-council-men and two commoners, fhall be fhut up in the town hall, without provifions, &c. till nine out of the twelve agree in the choice.

Its diftance from Newport is ten miles; but the road for pleafurable travelling is the worft in the ifland. There are not lefs than fifty-two gates to be paffed between the two places, which greatly adds to the irkfomnefs of it.

The river Yar prefents a beautiful en-

trance

trance, and takes a double courſe. The
branch to the ſouth-eaſt paſſes the valley before deſcribed, and ſaunters up to Tapnell;
a village ſituated at the bottom of Afton
downs. The other branch forms a more
conſiderable body, and ſeen from Freſhwater,
appears as a lake, the hills meeting, and the
ſhores projecting, ſo as to prevent the eye
from perceiving its communication with the
ſea.

The oppoſite ſhores of Norton, which form
the entrance of the river, are pleaſingly di-
verſified with broken grounds and groups
of trees; and likewiſe with interpoſing cottage roofs that break the too regular clumps.
It is navigable to the mills of Freſhwater,
where the bridge preſerves a ſufficient body
to add grandeur to the landſcape, and allow
ſcope for the pencil.

SECTION

SECTION IX.

HAVING refreſhed our horſes, we ſet out the ſame evening for Freſhwater Gate, taking the road that had brought us to Yarmouth from Linwood Green. We then ſtruck into the firſt right-hand road, leading to the bridge that croſſes the ſouth-eaſt courſe of the river.

Here the bridge became an object. From the hills adjoining to Yarmouth it is viewed to ſome advantage, but here it redoubled its harmony with the valley.—The ſun was warm and declining.—The ivy that had helped to deface its ſides, now brightened its appearance, and gave, as an atonement for its ravages, its friendly aid to bind the building, and variegate its general tints.—Nor did the hills in the diſtance diminiſh the ſplendor of the ſcene: a wood ſwept on the other ſide of the bridge from hill to hill, and formed a perfect amphitheatre.

The colouring was ſuperb and rich; a

glow

glow of purple ftained the diftance, while the faint rays of the fun juft caught the bridge, and glided along the tops of the wood. The fide-fcreens lay, one in a half tint, the oppofite one entirely in fhadow; the whole blending fo uniformly, that it had the moft pleafing effect we had feen in any view during our whole route.

At the declenfion of the fun, efpecially in the month of September, the grandeft effects of light and fhade are obfervable. The movement of thefe rapturous tranfits of Nature are inftantaneous; and if not clofely obferved, fly before the eye is half gratified. The colouring at this time is always chafte; and the length of the fhadows from the mountains, in general confine the light to a principal object; which, if it does not as quickly ftrike the imagination as its motion is hafty, every beauty muft inevitably be loft.

I am convinced that the remnants of light in an evening are much finer when the fun returns to the fouth, than when in the fpring it

it approaches the northern hemifphere. Nor does it lofe any of its luftre by fetting where the ocean conftitutes the horizon. In general its lights are clearer, and diffufe a greater variety of colours to the land; while the water, babbling up in gentle waves, catches its rays, and gives us the very foul and fpirit of *Claude*'s mafter pieces:

The evening drawing on, we haftened towards the intended fpot. Thorly furprized us when we entered it. From the maps of the ifland we had been led to expect that this parifh contained a confiderable village; but a few houfes only prefented themfelves, and thofe furrounded by woods. Wilmingham is a pleafant fpot, but nothing further.

From Afton we had a frefh view of the fcene we had had from the entrance of Yarmouth. The cliff of Frefhwater Gate rofe with majeftic grandeur, but from its chalky corner abruptly obtruded itfelf. The lines of Afton downs ranged beautifully; while the nobler afcent of the downs of Frefhwater doubled their fplendor; a gleam of

L 3   light

light ftole over the hills, and prefented the woody vale with force and bloom. The furzy fcrub that ftraggled on the furface of the mountains, was a great helpmate to foften their fides. The laft, but not the leaft addition to this view is the village on the oppofite fide of the water, whofe reflections gave every different hue to heighten the ftudy. We much regretted the want of a fore-ground, as nothing but a patch of ripe corn continually encountered the fight. Nor could we help wifhing for a few of thofe fcenes that prefented themfelves in the New Foreft; fome of its noble oaks would have fully completed the grandeur of the fcene before us.

We now afcended Afton down; and for the firft time had an uninterrupted view of the fea. The profpect was fine;—the evening was ferene;—and the billows, as if forgetful of their ufual boifteroufnefs, feemed to be lulled to a ftate of tranquillity by the warblings of the feathered fongfters in the neighbouring groves, whofe little throats poured forth, in moft melodious notes, their

grateful

grateful tranſports to the Great Giver of their daily food.—To add ſolemnity to the ſcene, the fluttering ſails of the ſurrounding veſſels lay motionleſs ; not admitted even the gentleſt breath of the zephyrs that wantoned about them.

On the right lay the ſpot called Freſhwater Gate, which, we were informed, derives its name from its being placed there to prevent the water of an adjacent ſpring from uniting with the ſea. This derivation, however, does not ſeem to be very well grounded.

A cottage is the only habitation to be found here, but that cottage, which is kept by a publican, affords every accommodation a traveller can wiſh for ; and frequent parties of pleaſure are made to it.

The cliffs that form Freſhwater-bay are very high, and when you look down from them, you find a degree of terror excited in the mind. Many parts of them, unable to withſtand the conſtant ravages of the ſea,

L 4   have

have been wafhed down. On the left hand
of the bay, two large maffes of the cliffs
have been torn from the fides, and have fallen perpendicularly into the water. In the
bottom of one of thefe fragments there is a
large chafm, forming a perfect arch; the
other appears to be ftill unhurt by the depredations of the fpray.

From this fpot St. Catherine's appears
the moft fouthern boundary of the ifland;
and owing to the chalky cliffs which are a-
bout half way up its fide on a platform of
green, is frequently taken for fome ancient
caftle. The fhore towards it is rocky, and
the cliffs exceedingly fteep, with fmall tufts
of grafs growing on their fides.

But when we viewed the cave of Frefhwater, we were loft in wonder at the dire-
ful effects of the raging foam. Thefe cliffs
meafure, from the furface of the fea at low
water to their top, near fix hundred feet.
The cave is a natural cavity in the bottom
of the rocks, forming two arches. Thofe
who vifit it can only enter at low water.
The

The infides of the arches are overgrown
with mofs and weeds, and ferve as a fine
contraft to the fea and cliffs. Several pieces
of rock, which have fallen from the afcents,
block up the paffage into the cave, at half
tide. Among thefe, one in particular, much
larger than the reft, rifes fome feet above
high-water mark; the form of which I have
particularly fketched, and it accompanies the
annexed view of this romantic fpot.

Stakes are faftened to the rocks, and others
are placed on the fhore, to which cords are
fixed, that paffing from ftem to ftern of the
boats belonging to the place, prevent them
from being beaten to pieces by the furf, or
carried to fea when the wind blows hard.
The bottom is a fine fand; and from the healthy fituation of the fpot, would be an excellent place to eftablifh a bathing machine; but
there being no houfes near, a confiderable
objection may arife from that circumftance.

On this fhore the naturalift will find
numerous attractions for his fcientific re-
fearches. A variety of foffils are impregnated
with

with the rocky fubftance of the cliffs, together with native fpars ;—copperas ftones are
frequently thrown by the tide on the beach;
—and pieces of iron ore, in its primitive
ftate, are fometimes ftrewed along the fhore.
Viens of rocks, fhooting from the cliffs, run
to a length that cannot be afcertained, into
the fea. At a diftance they appear like
water-pipes; and on examination are found
to confift in the middle of a vein of black
rock, covered with an incruftration of iron.
The fhape of thefe veins is fingular, but
very regular, and pointed; they dart into
the fea among the other rocks which form
the entrance of the cave.

Several cavities appeared to be in the rocks
as we viewed them towards the Needles,
but none of them led to a fubterraneous paffage of any length. There are three or four
at the bottom of the range called Main-
Bench, but none equal to Frefhwater-Cave.

Having made all the obfervations we could
on this bay, and the night creeping on apace,
we retired to the village; but not with any
                                                very

very fanguine hopes of meeting with agreeable accommodations. We, however, found
fuch as all thofe who are in purfuit of the
beauties of Nature, and can feaft on the delightful fcenes fhe prefents, will readily put
up with. To fuch, a favoury rafher, a flice
of brown bread, with a draught of home-
brewed beer, is a feaft;—the humble pallet,
a bed of down.

Wifhing to view a fun-rife on thefe hills,
we rofe by break of day; but fo different
are the morning and evening fcenes of the
ifland from thofe on the oppofite fhores,
that it is fcarcely to be credited, unlefs you
narrowly watch every operation of Nature.
We expected to have feen the fun burft from
behind the eaftern hills, and immediately
fcatter the dewy fubftances that fall in great
profufion here; but inftead of viewing his
rays contending only with the morning va-
pours, as the day broke, a thick condenfed
cloud reared itfelf from the fouth-eaft, and
continued to increafe in its fize, till it enve-
loped all the hills in a gloomy fhade. Short-
ly after, a glimmering ray of light fkirted
the

the horizon, and diffused its beams to every point, but that in so weak and faint a manner as was far from pleafing. From its earlieft approach, at the dawning of the day, we had entertained hopes of feeing the fun gild the tops of the mountains with all its brilliance, and break with grandeur on the neighbouring copfe; but in this we were difappointed. We were informed by the farmers refident here, that they fcarcely ever knew the day break in this manner, with clouds accompanying the opening dawn, but that the enfuing day proved very hot. For once, however, they were miftaken: during this day the rain frequently defcended on our heads in torrents.

Allum Bay was our route on the fucceeding day; where our expectations were not in the leaft degree difappointed. In our way to it, feveral confined views, at the foot of the mountains, had much the fame appearance as the Cumberland and Weftmorland hills give to a picture—a ftone-fided cottage, with one-half of the roof flated, the

other

other covered with a moſſy thatch, ſurrounded by pleaſing clumps of trees and
projections of rocks from the overgrown
ferny heath;—while a ſhattered gate bounds
ſome nearly-ruined ſtony wall, that incloſes
a flock of ſheep, and confines them upon the
rugged ſteep.

Scenes of this kind frequently ſkirted the
road's ſide till we reached the ſummit of the
path that led to the warren. Here a new
ſcene ruſhed upon us, as pleaſing as it was
picturefque. The declivities of the valley
was a fine ſpecimen of broken ground;—
the burrows of the little inhabitants of
the warren added relief to the rocks and
verdure that adorned its ſides;—and a mixture of gravel and marle, with here and
there maſſes of white ſand, contributed to
the perfection that was viſible to every
difcriminating eye;—while the Needles terminated the firſt fight, the Iſle of Portland
compoſed the greateſt diſtance.

As we deſcended the road, a horſe, tied
to a buſh, obſtructed our progreſs. Suppoſing

pofing it to belong to fome vifitor, like ourfelves, of thefe picturefque fcenes, who,
finding the hill too fteep, and the road too
rugged, to ride down with fafety, had dif-
mounted and walked down, we followed the
example he had fet us :—but what was our
furprife when, coming up with the owner
of the horfe, we recognized him to be my
worthy friend, Mr. La Porte, a very ingenious artift !

Before our arrival, this gentleman had
ranfacked the fpot; and did not hefitate
to pronounce the fight equal to any he had
ever feen, either in or out of the ifland
we were upon. As from the nature of
our plan, our fpecimens of this place muft
fall very fhort of the numberlefs beauties
it exhibits, for a more extenfive reprefent-
ation of them we will beg leave to refer
our readers to the works of the before-mentioned artift; from whofe chafte and correct pencil every beauty, juftly and pleafingly delineated, may be expected ; and,
from his rapturous exclamations when on
the fpot, we are not without hopes that the

next

next exhibition at the Royal Academy will be graced with them.

The mountainous cliffs that form Allum Bay are terrific in the extreme; a huge angle of rock, fhelving over your head, is the conftant accompaniment of the heights; and many of them are near feven hundred feet from the furface of the fea at low water.

In thefe rocks the progreffive operations of nature in their formation are eafily dif-cernible.—We found them to be compofed of a regular gradation of fubftances, from a watery clay to a perfect and fubftantial petrefaction. The winter blafts, and in-ceffant ravages of the fea, frequently hurl large tufts of earth from the ftupendous heights to the ftrand beneath; and thefe, lying there immovable, gather from the undulations of the waves fmall fhells, fof-fils, and pieces of flint; till, hardened by time and the petrifying quality of the water, they become at length a perfect fubftance.

We

We broke feveral large clumps, which had undergone this tranfmutation, and found that they had attracted every marine production. In their primary ftate they appeared to have been chiefly clay, without any durability. Their fecond ftate was, when the water had thrown its floating weeds round their fides, and had juft begun to attract the foffil particles and pieces of broken fhells, which, entangling in the mofs and fegments, there remained, and contributed to their growing ftrength. In their third progreffion we found, that flint and fpar had forced their way into their centre, and cemented the earth together, till, in the courfe of time, the water had petrified, and clothed them with copperas ftones and iron ore for their outward coat. Their fourth and laft ftage was, where, the waves having wafhed them every tide, they plainly exhibited, on their outward appearance, all the foregoing fubftances entirely converted to hard folid rock. The minutenefs with which we examined thefe ftones left us not the leaft room to doubt but that falt water is pof-

feffed

feffed of the power to petrify, in a feries of time, the fofteft and moft diffoluble affemblage of earths.

The fine white fand before mentioned is found here, about a hundred feet above the furface of the beach, of a peculiar quality. The ftratum lies between two others of clay. This fand is the only fort that is to be found in thefe kingdoms fit for making white glafs ; it is likewife ufed at Worcefter for manufacturing china; nor will any other do for thefe ufes. The miners employed in digging it informed us, that this vein, from repeated examinations, has been found to run entirely through, from the extremity of the point oppofite to Yarmouth to the downs of Afton. It belongs to Mr. Urry, of Yarmouth, and the profit arifing from it is very confiderable. As often as the weather will permit, veffels lie in Allum Bay to load with it.—Here likewife is dug the tobacco pipe clay before fpoken of.

The compofitions of the foil which form thefe ftupendous heights are of the greateft

Vol. I.   M   variety

variety we ever met with—The bottom is
a hard mixture of flint and chalk, whose
durability is able to encounter any attacks
but the ocean's fury. The next vein is a
black softish mud, or watery clay, over
which is an ochre of a bright cast. Here
the sand-pits take their rise, whose stra-
tum, measuring ten feet in depth, is situated on the hard plain floor of ochre before mentioned, having above it another
vein of much the same quality. Over
these we observed a variety of coloured
clays and earths, some of which were of
a perfect pink and green hue, with the
interposition of chalk, flint, and mould,
without distinction. In short, I scarcely
think that any part of the kingdom produces, in so small a compass, such a mixture of soils.

The workmen are seldom able to conti-
nue working at the sand-pits longer than
the month of October; sometimes not so
long. In the winter, the sea, agitated by
the violent south-west winds, which then
generally blow, breaks into the pits, and,

under-

undermining the other heights, brings
down the whole force of the mountain.
When thefe crafhes happen, they may be
diftinctly heard at the village of Frefhwater, though two miles diftant.

This fufficiently accounts for the great
quantities of rock that bind the fhores.
When they fall to the water's edge, every
tide, as before obferved, adds permanency
to their fubftance. A little nearer to the
chalky fides of Frefhwater downs we ftill
found greater cavities in the earth. The
quantity of rain that in this part fweeps
along the downs, here finds a vent. The
day being rainy and boifterous, we enjoyed
peculiar fatisfaction from viewing the ravages inceffantly committed by it.—A bold
ftream iffued from the top of the rocks,
which joined feveral fmaller ones about a
quarter of the way down; where, violently
burfting on the large clumps of iron ore
from which the earth had been wafhed,
they gave grandeur and beauty to the
fcene. When the torrents caufed by the
rain are very violent, they carry all before

M 2   them

them from the heights, leaving their im-
pregnations on the furface of the earth.
Large maffes, of a green colour, appeared
on many of the points, which we fuppofed
to have been caufed by the quantity of
copperas that lies on the rocks; and we
likewife found feveral ftones ftrongly in-
fufed with a tincture of that mineral.

Nor are thefe cliffs deficient in iron; feveral fprings iffue from the fides of them,
which, in their paffage to the fea, leave a
fediment behind them tinctured with it.
A great quantity of iron ore lies along the
beach, which, like the rocks before defcribed, had received additional ftrength
from having been expofed to the air and
fea. Some of thefe we found as foft as
clay, and many harder than the rocks
themfelves; for, on oppofing their ftrength,
the iron remained whole, while the rocks
chipped in pieces.

Thefe rocks and earths, when the water
leaves them, appear very like the Glaciere
mountains, in Switzerland; feveral hundred

dred points fhoot upwards, gradually de-
creafing in their circumference. We obferved that the fprings, even when not augmented by the rain, formed two or three
cafcades ; and thefe, at the time we viewed
them, were by no means contemptible ones,
We thought them fo interefting that we
took the annexed view of them. But it
muft be obferved, that as thefe fcenes, from
the before-mentioned devaftations, alter
every year, they may not perhaps be
found exactly in the fame pofition as when
viewed by us. Whether they are or no,
it is certain they will not be feen to lefs
advantage, as every fummer adds frefh,
though tranfient beauties to them.

The time to fee them in their greateft
perfection muft be while the fun is fetting ; his beams then giving additional
force to every touch Nature fo wantonly
fports with ; as they ftand at the clofe of the
day directly in his focus.

We now paffed along the beach, ftill
nearer to the white borders of the Nee-

dles,

dles, where frefh objects enchanted our
fight. A ftupendous afcent, near five hundred feet in height, with another rather
lefs, one of them of a perfect pink colour,
the other of a bright ochre with its foot
covered with the green fediment of copperas, had an appearance as wonderful as
uncommon. So fudden a difference, though
fingular, muft, when blended in a picture,
produce a charming harmony. The only
ftiff object was the white cliffs; but the
glare of thefe was rather alleviated by the
weeds which hung down them, and the
blue furface of the flints.

The point that extends to thofe fatal
rocks, called the Needles, (which once,
there is not the leaft room to doubt, formed the extremity of the land,) is near a
quarter of a mile in length. From its
fides flow feveral ftreams, but they are too
fmall to form a body. The quality of the
water of thefe ftreams is allowed, by feveral gentlemen who have analized it, to be
very good. They are chiefly chalybeate;
but one we tafted left the rancorous flavour

of

of copperas behind. It was not, however, sufficient to affect the ftomach. There is every probability that this long wafte will in time become, like the Needles, a terror to feamen; but it will require many centuries to bring fo grand an object to perfection.

As we returned, a number of fmall ftones rattled down from the fides of the rocks, which we thought, at firft, were thrown by fome playfome boys who were above; but we foon found it was occafioned by the fheep that were grazing on the very brink of the precipice, fome of whom had even got below the edge, in order to pick up the herbs that fkirt its brow.

The only inhabitants of this dreadful promontory are gulls and puffings, who refort to it about the month of May, to breed, and leave it towards September. The country people refident in this part of the ifland are very dexterous in taking the eggs of thefe birds. This they do by means of an iron crow, which they fix

M 4   into

into the ground on the top of the cliffs, and
fufpending themfelves from it, in a bafket
faftened to a rope, they get at the nefts.——
A method not unlike that purfued by the
gatherers of famphire, from the fide of
Dover Cliff, as defcribed by Shakefpeare,
in his King Lear:

" ———— Half way down
" Hangs one that gathers famphire;—dreadful trade?
" Methinks, he feems no bigger than his head."

As foon as the men get thus fufpended,
they halloo; upon which the birds quit
the holes wherein their eggs are depofited,
and, flying away, leave them a prey to the
unfeeling plunderer. The eggs of thefe
birds are found here in great plenty, and
this is the only part of the coaft where
they build. Some of them make even
the Needles a receptacle for their young.
Strangers frequently buy thefe eggs
through curiofity; but they are feldom
eaten, except by the country people who
take them, and who likewife fometimes
deftroy the birds for the fake of their
feathers,

feathers, by knocking them down with sticks as they fly out of their holes.

The chief food of these birds is fish, which they take with extraordinary agility, picking them up as they skim along the surface of the sea. The puffing is a species of the seagull, differing from it only in colour, its head and wings being promiscuously covered with brown spots.— Many gentlemen resort to these cliffs, in order to enjoy the amusement of shooting; and as, upon hearing the report of the gun, several hundreds of the birds leave their holes at a time, and hover about, they generally find excellent sport.

At Lymington the Needles have a very pleasing appearance, not unlike that which St. Catherine's makes when seen from Freshwater gate. The singular effects that time has wrought on the beach of these celebrated rocks, was the last thing which engaged our attention.—The pebbles and flints lying on the surface of it, are perfectly smooth, from the repeated friction of the

the waves, and the force with which the sea dashes them against each other; so that they appear exactly like a great number of marbles, only of a more confiderable fize. Here likewife many veins of iron, refembling water-pipes, like thofe at Frefhwater gate, before defcribed, launch a long way into the fea; and, although the bottom is fandy, it requires a thorough knowledge of the coaft to land clear of the rocky parts.

The weeds, called here by the country people delfe and tangle, grow and flourifh on thefe rocks; and they are likewife fuperbly touched with a bright yellow mofs, which adds relief to the other tints that ftrew the fhore. Allum is alfo found here, but in no great quantity, nor very good in its quality. From this circumftance we may fuppofe the bay to have received its name.

SECTION

SECTION X.

WE now left this place, but not without great regret, having received
inexpreſſible pleaſure from its tremendous
grandeur ; of which we have endeavoured
to give our readers ſome idea in the annexed plate. Having mounted our horſes,
and being joined by the gentleman we had
accidentally fallen in with, we ſat out with
a deſign to aſcend the downs of Freſhwater ; but miſſing the road, we attempted to climb the mountain. The ſlippery-
neſs, however, of the graſs, occaſioned by
the rain and the ſteepneſs of its ſides, prevented us from carrying this deſign into
execution. We accordingly diſmounted,
and, with great difficulty, regained the
road. And we would take this opportunity
to caution all thoſe who viſit the Iſle of
Wight, not, in any part of it, to leave
the beaten road, if they can poſſibly avoid
it ; for though the people of the country,
who are not eaſily terrified at any intrica-
cies, can readily find the neareſt way from

place

place to place over the downs, yet if you do not perceive a track to lead up the hill, you may be affured there is no paffable road that way.

Having regaled ourfelves at Frefhwater gate, we again mounted the downs of Afton. From the extreme height of thefe plains, and of the adjacent ones, we gener-ally found the fummits of them barren, while the vallies are exceedingly fruitful; and where the hills are cultivated, and grain fown, from the almoft continual north-eaft winds that fweep over them in the winter, and their being expofed to the fcorching rays of the fun in the fummer, (a contraft unfavourable to vegetation,) we often ob-ferved, that while a part of it was green, the reft was ftunted and parched up. This difference in the ripenefs, together with the fmallnefs of the ear, even in its higheft per-fection, renders the cultivation of corn on thefe elevated fpots very unprofitable, and not worthy of the farmer's attention.

They, however, afford a fweet and rich pafture

pafture for fheep, and fome are kept upon
them ; yet not fo many as there might be ;
nor is it in the power of argument to prevail on the farmers to extend fo beneficial
a branch. The fheep in thefe parts appear
to be of the Dorfetfhire breed—tall, and
well fleeced ;—and the mutton is equal in
goodnefs to any in Great Britain.

Wifhing to keep as clofe to the fea fhore
as poffible, we now made for Compton
Chine ; but met with nothing interefting
till we croffed Compton Down ; we then
came to a fmall village, called Brook.
The chine of Brook has a greater chafm
to prefent than Compton ; but even this
did not come up to our expectations.
The village of Brook lies in a recefs formed by two mountains, which fhelter it from
the violence of the winds.

The places to which, in thefe parts,
the name of *chine* is given, are breaks or
chafms in the cliffs, which feem to have
been occafioned by fome violent eruption

or

or infringement of the ocean. Through
fome of them we obferved fprings to flow.

From Brook we croffed to Mottifton ; and
in our way paffed through a foil entirely
different from any we had hitherto feen.
For near two miles the furface of the road
confifted of fand, perfectly red. Under this
was a vein of white fand. And beneath
that a great quantity of iron ore, intermixed
with flint and chalk.

The variation of the foil in this ifland is
beyond defcription. They may be truly
termed the vagaries of Nature; in which
fhe fports with uncontrolled extravagance.
Every year, to an obfervant and frequent
vifitor of the ifland, fhe prefents fomething
new ; and in every alteration fhe feems to
be more luxuriant. To-day we find her
thrufting forth fome bold promontory into
the fea, in order to check the impetuous
waves, and afford the mariner an afylum
from their fury. To-morrow, unmindful
of the magnificence of her former work, fhe
hurls the foaming wave againft its ftately

fide,

fide, and levels it with the humbler fhore;
and probably after having tumbled this
precipice headlong down its craggy fteep,
fhe forms a rugged ftony channel for fome
rapid torrent, produced by the heavy rains
that fo frequently annoy the weftern coafts
of England; which rufhing down its fide,
forms at once maffes for the artift, and prefents a pleafing fight to the curious fpec-
tator.

The hills of Yarmouth, as well as the
vallies of Newtown and Shalfleet, were no
longer vifible, as we proceeded to Mottifton,
being intercepted by the Brixton mountains,
which, from their height, except directly in
the road-way, are utterly impaffable. The
village of Mottifton is a very defirable fpot,
pleafantly fituated, and commanding charming views of the fea. The church is antique,
but almoft robbed of its grandeur by the
modern mode of beautifying we have fo often cenfured.

About half a mile from the village, after
we had left it, a fcene prefented itfelf that
struck

ſtruck us with ſurprize and admiration. The
village, behind us, which is almoſt ſurrounded by woods, juſt opened ſufficient to preſent its church, ſpire, and entrance; together with an old houſe of ſtone, which the
ſun caught full upon ;—the trees lying in
ſhadow, formed the fore-ground ;—while
the diſtant cliffs of Freſhwater, Main Bench,
and Scratchel's Bay, cloſed upon the verdure
of the wood which ſurrounded the village,
and brought it out ;—the relief was aſtoniſh-
ing, and the ſight peculiarly pleaſing. The
ſea lay in ſhadow in the diſtance ; and ſeveral veſſels, with light glancing on their top-
ſails, finiſhed the view.

Such ſcenes frequently encounter the eye
here, but fall infinitely ſhort when deſcribed,
of what they are in reality. To pourtray
them in their own glowing colours is not in
the power of my pen or pencil; to point out
ſuch as are moſt ſtriking, and to give a de-
ſcription as nearly adequate as poſſible, is
the utmoſt I can do.

The downs of Brixton on our left often
afforded

afforded fine back-grounds. A number of rocks ſtart from the brows of the hills, the moſs and graſs charmingly blending on their ſurface. A few patches of white, occaſioned by holes which the ſheep had made to lie in, were rather diſguſting to the ſight. From the very great height of the rocks, the ſheep that grazed on the brows of them appeared like dots of white; they, however, when they grouped, ſtrongly heightened the effect. There was a littleneſs in the valley before us, occaſioned by ſeveral aukward clumps of ill-grown trees, that broke the fine ſweeps it took. The hill of St. Catherine's and Appuldurcombe terminated the view. Black Down alſo preſented its loftineſs, and added to the ſcene.

We left Pitt Place and Chilton Chine to the right, and paſſed on to Brixton, or, as it is called here, Briſon. The corruption of this proper name renders it neceſſary for me to mention, that the names of places are not uncommonly corrupted in theſe parts. Nay, if you enquire the road to any place, calling it as it is uſually writ-

ten, the odds are confiderably againft you,
but that they tell you there is no fuch place.
Even the people of Newport indulge themfelves in thefe liberties ; fo that unlefs you
have a map with you to rectify their mif-
nomers, you are very often at a lofs how to
proceed.

Brixton is one of the largeft villages in
this part of the ifland, and, in my opinion,
one of the pleafanteft. The road through
it is clean, and kept in good order. It is
conveniently fituated, in point of diftance,
from the bay to which it gives name. The
parifh church belonging to it ftands towards the fkirts of the village ; but this
alfo has had the iron hand of embellifh-
ment laid on it. A ftream paffes through
this place, which takes it rife near Mottifton, and empties itfelf into the bay at Jack-
man's Chine. At the bottom of the village, as
we courfed its fides, we obferved this brook
to widen, when it afforded a pleafing effect.

The inundation of the fea, completing
what fome eruption had begun, forms here
                                    a fhort

a fhort declivity, overgrown with fcrubby bufhes. There is alfo a boat-houfe here, where feveral boats are kept in readinefs to affift the unfortunate mariners, in cafe of fhipwrecks, which are not unfrequent on this coaft. The bay, as to its appearance, affords nothing very pleafing to the fight; every wave, however, that broke upon its beach, where there is a conftant furf, brought a charm with it.

This furf we foon viewed in all its terrors; for the morning turning hazy, a ftorm commenced, which obliged us to take fhelter in the boat-houfe. From hence we faw the fea, with its wonted fury, waging war with the more peaceable cliff; while the torrent, in wild career, rufhing from the heights down the clay and ftony fteep, forced its way through the foaming billows, and tinctured with its ftreams the borders of the bay.

After waiting an hour, by which time the ftorm was abated, we again fet forward, with a determination to fkirt the

N 2   boundaries

boundaries of the cliffs which lay neareſt to the ſea. Several receſſes obtrude themſelves on the land, but without producing that terrific effect we had frequently ſeen them do.

We ſwept round the Bay of Brixton, but received no very great pleaſure from viewing its formal plains. On our left we obſerved Black Down to open, and preſent us with a view of Culver Cliffs, which lie at the eaſtern extremity of the iſland. The vallies throughout the iſland frequently form a curve round the foot of ſome dreadful precipice, and lead your ſight to the moſt beautiful ſcenes. We were here gratified with one of theſe; which, diſdaining all bounds, began its opening at Sandown, to the eaſtward, and turning round the foot of St. Catherine's, joined the vallies of Brixton and Chale, and from thence ran on to Freſhwater. Notwithſtanding we were now on the loweſt part of the iſland, we had a very plain and diſtinct view of its extremeſt bounds.

It

It may be neceffary to remark, for the benefit of thofe who vifit thefe parts, that, in going round this coaft, great inconvenience attends keeping clofe to the fea; as the road over the downs is impaffable for carriages, and even very troublefome to thofe on horfeback; there being near fifty gates between Frefhwater gate and St. Catherine's, and thofe of the worft kind. In almoft every field we were obliged to difmount, in order to cut the cords by which they were faftened, otherwife we fhould not have been able to have proceeded.

Continuing our route, we came to Barns Hole, which might properly be deemed a chine. As the operations of Nature in the formation of works of this kind admit of many hypothefes, I fhall give my opinion of it with diffidence. Barns Hole is a vaft chafm in the earth, fronting the fea, which extends a confiderable way towards Brixton; and, as you enter it, infpires the mind with horror. The entrance has the appearance of leading to fome fubterraneous paffage, which furnifhes a retreat for a neft of rob-

N 3

bers

bers. The fides of it are four hundred feet high, meafured from the water, and are coated on the outfide with a difmal black earth, which confirms the terror impreffed on the imagination by the firft view of it. It is furrounded by a loathfome, unfruitful foil, and fcarcely a fhrub cares to cling to its fteep afcents. A ftream paffes through it that empties itfelf into the fea.

The reflections that arofe in our minds on viewing fuch a combination of ftriking effects, were, that they muft have been occafioned by fome great convulfion of Nature; who, being internally overloaded, difcharged the extraneous matter by fome terrible eruption. This fuppofition feems to be confirmed by the quantity of minerals, and the variety of foils, that are found about it. Several fpecimens of fulphurous matter, though not very ftrongly impregnated, lay on the fhore.

SECTION

SECTION XI.

WE now made our way towards Atherfield Point, leaving the village of
Atherfield, and also Kingftone, to the left.
A great noblenefs of valley extends all the
way to Chale; but it is too much cultivated
to afford an artift fatisfaction.

Still continuing on the downs, we came
to that point of Chale Bay which is called
Atherfield Point, traverfing nearly the fame
kind of foil and country we had hitherto
done. The hills of St. Catherine began
now to form a noble appearance. At
Frefhwater, as we obferved before, they
looked like caftles; here they appeared
like fortreffes of great ftrength. From the
regular breaks in the rocks, and thefe being
not unlike gun-ports, or embrafures, they
might, about twilight, be eafily miftaken for
fuch.

Its heights are grand and picturefque,
and they clearly prove that this ifland,

N 4

with

with regard to its formation, has every advantage; for where the fea would, from the part being moft expofed to its fury, have committed a breach, the land, boldly rifing, protects it from every inundation. And, if we may judge from what the inhabitants fay of it, the Ifle of Wight has fcarcely its equal in the world.—Its land (fay they) is fertile; its hufbandmen induftrious; its females prolific; its hills a fure protection from the devaftations of the fea; its coafts too rocky to admit the approach of an enemy; and, above all, its inhabitants chearful, good tempered, and hofpitable; all uniting in the wifh and endeavour to render their ifland attractive in every refpect to ftrangers.

I muft here remark, that the parts of the ifland we were before fpeaking of, are fo unlike the eaftern fhores, in point of appearance, that was a perfon to be fuddenly tranfported from one part to the other, I am of opinion he would fcarcely believe he were upon the fame ifland.

We

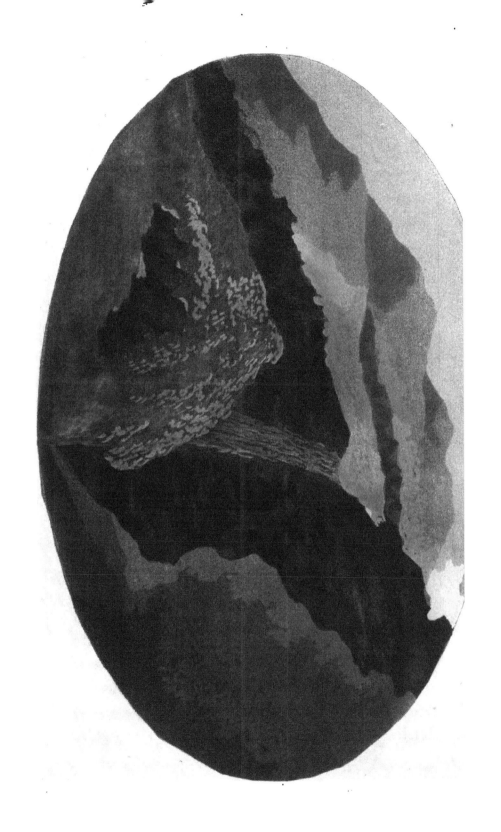

We now paſſed Walpan Chine, and another ſmall infringement of the ocean, where
are a few huts belonging to ſome boatmen
and fiſhermen, which ſeverely feel the ra-
vaging effeƈts of the ſea. About the middle
of Chale Bay, on the top of the cliffs, there
ſtands a houſe, which appears to have been
ereƈted for the reception of travellers ; but
at the time we paſſed it, it was locked up ;
ſo that we could procure no refreſhment.

We now arrived at one of thoſe cavities
before deſcribed, called Black-Gang Chine,
which we were informed received its name
from a gang of pirates who formerly made
it their place of reſidence ; and its appearance ſeems fully to confirm this ſuppoſition;
for it is far more dreadful to behold than
thoſe mentioned in the foregoing ſeƈtions.
The ſize of the chaſm, and its tremendous
ſhelving rocks, cannot fail of inſpiring the
mind with horror. The imagination, while
viewing it, may almoſt lead the inquiſitive
traveller to fancy that the earth had juſt
opened her horrid jaws, and, from the very
ſpot on which he then ſtood, had entombed

in

in her bowels fome unwary traveller, who,
like himfelf, was prying into the wonderful
operations of Nature.—I never beheld fo
awful a fight as thefe ponderous fteeps exhibit. The fides of the chafm, which are
little fhort of five hundred feet high, are
fhelving, and many parts of the top are
overfpread with fhrubs.

On its fummit a fpring takes its rife, and
winds flowly down to the fea. The flow-
nefs of its courfe prevents it from proving
detrimental to the cliffs. The water iffuing
from this fpring is of a peculiar nature.
It acts as a gentle aperient. When firft
poured into a bottle, it is as clear as cryftal;
but after remaining in it fome time, a very
confiderable fediment appears at the bottom.
We feparated fome of this fediment, and
found it to contain particles of iron ore,
which emitted a fulphurous fmell. Several
copperas ftones lay about, efpecially in the
ftreams proceeding from the fprings, which
feemed to be in their native ftate. Some
fpecimens of rock allum were likewife
ftrewed

ftrewed around, but not in the fame profufion as at Allum Bay.

Many fhips have fatally experienced the
deftructive effects of the rocks that line
Chale Bay.—They juft lurk underneath the
furface of the water, and, in conjunction
with the Cape of Rocken End, occafion
very heavy fwells, efpecially if the wind
be foutherly. When the tide runs ftrong,
and the wind is fouth-weft, if a veffel is
not far enough to the fouthward to weather
the point of St. Catherine's, fhe is fure to
be upon the rocks. It is ftill within the
remembrance of many, that, during one
tempeftuous night, not lefs than fourteen
fail met their fate in this dangerous bay:
and fcarcely a winter paffes but what accidents of the fame kind happen. But as
for fome years paft boats have been kept in
readinefs, and men are conftantly attending to afford every affiftance upon fuch occafions, many lives have been preferved.

We are forry, however, to be obliged to
add, that the favage cuftom of plundering
wrecks,

wrecks, and ſtripping the dead, whenever theſe accidents happen, too much prevails among the country people reſident on the weſtern coaſt. Deaf to the calls of Humanity, theſe unfeeling wretches hear with unconcern the cries of the ſhipwrecked mariner, ſtruggling with the boiſterous waves; or ſee the beauteous corſe of ſome fair paſſenger lying lifeleſs on the beach, perhaps ſtill preſſing a beloved infant to her boſom. Intent only on ſecuring their ill-got property, they cannot beſtow a thought on the unfortunate; nor will one among them ſuffer a tender ſenſation to make its way to his heart.

To procure a reſtoration of the property thus inhumanly obtained, or to bring theſe lawleſs plunderers to juſtice, is equally impracticable; as every one ſhares in the plunder, it is the intereſt of every individual to unite in concealing or defending it.

The ſalvage uſually allowed for ſaving merchandize from ſhips wrecked, may ſometimes be thought worth attention, and

and be the means of protecting it from avaricious depredators; but as it is seldom that any emolument arifes from the prefervation of lives, little attention is in general paid to that point. Were a premium to be offered by government for every perfon preferved from a fhipwrecked veffel, and a medal, as a badge of diftinction, added to it by fome great perfonage; or was a fociety to be eftablifhed for the promotion of fo benevolent a purpofe; many that now perifh for want of needful affiftance, might be reftored to ufefulnefs and fociety.

It has been known that the moft daring exertions on thefe occafions have met with a very inadequate reeompence.—An inftance of this kind is ftill talked of in the Ifle of Wight. At the time the Juno, a Dutch frigate, was loft on this coaft, a fmuggler, with four other perfons, ventured out to her affiftance, notwithftanding they were in the extremeft danger from the violence of the furf, which every inftant made its way over the boat. They, however, at length gained the fhip, and brought off, and fafely landed

landed the whole of the crew, except three perfons, who were wafhed off the raft. And for a deed which Britifh feamen alone could have accomplifhed ;—a deed worthy of the higheft praife, and the moft ample remune-ration ;—the only recompence they received was a paltry ten pound bank note.—Can we wonder then that fuch exertions are not more frequently heard of ?

We could not pafs the fatal fpot where fo many brave feamen, the fupport and glory of this commercial kingdom, find an un-timely grave, without heaving a figh ; and, at the fame time indulging a wifh that fome method may be devifed to prevent every avoidable decreafe of fo valuable a body of men.

Leaving this gloomy track, we proceeded to the village of Chale, which lies about a mile to the left of the Chine, and is but a fmall and irregular place. The church, which was founded during the reign of Henry the Firft, is, in the tower part, very much like that of Carifbrook, but not fo large.

As

As you afcend the hill beyond it, looking back, the valley toward Frefhwater appears very extenfive;—Brixton down binds the right-hand fcreens;—the ocean diminifhes to the left;—while the cliffs at the Needles clofe the land view, and in fome degree foften the formal valley. Too great a number of unpleafing lines range down the dale, which throws a ftiffnefs over it.

The people of the ifland call it a garden; and fo it really is; but in too great a degree to pleafe an amateur of the true picturefque. This part of the ifland, as to its appearance, differs very much from the northern part, which is occafioned by a want of wood to give a variegation to its colours. A famenefs runs through the whole, the downs of Brixton excepted, which in fome parts are fcrubby, with broken ground; but in this not equal to what we afterwards faw on the eaft-fide of St. Catherine's.

From Chale we mounted St. Catherine's Hill, which we found far fteeper than any we had hitherto met with; and nearly the whole way was not very fafe for a horfe.

The

The road lies on the fide of a precipice, at leaft three hundred feet high, and tremendous to look down; the oppofite fide is bounded by a bank. After fome difficulty we at length attained its fummit.

This hill is faid to be the higheft in the ifland; but whether it is fo we will not take upon ourfelves to fay; as, after frequent experiments, fuch as comparing it with the appearance of the other hills, we ftill remained in doubt.

Stories are told by the inhabitants of the parifh of Chale of the finking of Week down, which lies about three miles off, in the intermediate way between St. Catherine's and Shanklin down. They fay, that formerly Shanklin down, through the interference of Week down, could only be feen from St. Catherine's; whereas now it is vifible from Chale down; confequently either Week down muft have funk confiderably, or Shanklin down muft have increafed its altitude. And fome of the old people tell you that this has partly happened within their

own

own remembrance. So wonderful are the operations of Nature, that it is not for man to fay, " It cannot be ;" but this is an event fo far out of her ufual courfe, that I own I could not readily give credit to it.

On the top of St. Catherine's is a light-houfe, and a beacon, neither of which are now ufed. The tower ferves, in the day time, for an excellent land-mark ; it being near eight hundred feet above the level of the fea at low water. A fmall part of the chapel is remaining ; it is in for man octa-gon, and by fome called the hermitage, from the circumftance of a prieft's having formerly immured himfelf in it from the world.

As we examined the infide of this place of holy retirement, the ftory of Dr. Gold-fmith's Hermit inftantly occurred to our re-membrance, and impreffed itfelf on our minds. The hearth whereon he had once trimmed the chearful embers ; the wicket ; and many other circumftances, led us to fancy that this might have been the fpot where Edwin had taken up his abode; and that the pleafing tale owed its birth to the Hermitage of St. Catherine's. The wilder- nefs alone was wanting to complete the ima- gined fcene.

The views from the hill are very exten- five, and likewife reminded us of that ele- gant and natural poet who, in his "Travel- ler," from among the Alpine folitudes looks down, and thus exclaims:

" Ye glittering towns, with wealth and fplendor crown'd,
" Ye fields, where fummer fpreads profufion round,
" Ye lakes, whofe veffels catch the bufy gale,
" Ye bending fwains, that drefs the flow'ry vale,
" For me your tributary ftores combine;
" Creation's tenant, all the world is mine."

We had from hence a complete view round the ifland, except in one point, which was interrupted by the downs of Brixton, thefe lying too near the fight.—To the weft, the iflands of Purbec and Portland were very diftinguifhable;—the land towards Lyming- ton feemed almoft to join the ifland; a fmall part of the channel by which it is fe- parated being vifible, but barely fufficient to let you fee what it was;—the New Foreft

reared

reared its oaks on the hills, and ranged to
the mouth of Hampton water;—the point
towards Monckton fort was perfectly confpicuous, and the hills of Portfdown clofed
its extent;—we could alfo fee land at a very
great diftance to the eaftward; and it is af-
firmed by fome, that the point which forms
the bay of Brighton, is to be perceived
from hence.

The Culver cliffs bound another valley,
which, as before obferved, joins Brixton dale.
The woody defcents of Ride feemed to flope
gradually to the water's edge, and foftened
the harfher lines of the mountains.

On the fide of the hill of St. Catherine's
that lies towards the fea, the defcent is quite
perpendicular, 'till interrupted by a fmall
flat green of no confiderable width, when it
again defcends in the fame abrupt manner,
to the water's edge. The river Medina takes
its rife at the foot of this hill, and after paffing through Newport, empties itfelf into
the fea at Cowes. The fources from whence
the river originates, are fecured by this hill

O 2   from

from any inundation of the fea; which the
inhabitants fay was never known to happen
on any part of their coafts, except during
the winter months, in a fmall degree at
Gurnet bay.

When we defcended the hill, an odd circumftance attracted our notice, which though
trivial in itfelf, we mention, as it may appear as fingular to our readers as it did to
us. It being harveft time, a chearfulnefs
and jollity feemed to prevail at a farm-houfe
we paffed at the bottom of the hill, which
did not extend to the whole of the inhabitants; for we obferved that a fine game cock
and his feathered mate walked about in a
melancholy mood. Inftead of " proudly
ftrutting before his dame to the ftack, or
the barn door," as the cock defcribed by
Milton did, poor Chanticleer went flowly on,
with a large piece of flat ftick faftened to his
breaft, followed by his folitary companion,
dame Partlet, who had a clog tied to her leg,
of the fame kind as thofe fixed on the legs
of horfes, though not fo large. And this
was done we found to prevent their entering
the

the fields, and committing depredations on the newly reaped corn. We foon after faw feveral others hampered nearly in the fame manner.—A fight, at once fo droll and fo novel, afforded us no little entertainment.

From St. Catherine's we croffed the common fields to Niton, which is frequently termed Crab Niton, from the great number of crabs found on that coaft. The want of a good road to this village makes the vifiting it very inconvenient to travellers. The foil here is of a different nature from what we had hitherto paffed; it appeared to confift of a fine mould, without any mixture of its favourite accompaniment, chalk.

From the top of St. Catherine's this village prefents itfelf as one of the neareft; Godfill, Brixton, Mottifton, Chale, Kingfton, and feveral others are alfo within fight.

The village of Niton has nothing of novelty to attract attention, nor has it even pleafantnefs of fituation to boaft; it being entirely immured between two hills, fo that

O 3　　　　　there

there is neither a view of the fea, nor a good land profpect to be had from it. There is a neat brick houfe in it belonging to the Rev. Mr. Barwis, which is the only one worthy of notice; all the reft are cottages, intermixed with a few farm-houfes.

From hence we took the right-hand road to Buddle; where a part of the cliffs break up, and form the commencement of thofe called Under Cliff. The appearance of this immenfe pile of rocks is noble, picturefque, and grand; and fo fpacious are they, that the downs of Chale are fupported by them. All the broken rocky parts, which have been feparated from the main body, are over-grown with fhrubs, and fweetly foften their rugged texture. Several cottages rear their heads from among the bufhes, and, by contrafting Art with Nature in its rudeft ftate, fhows to great advantage the romantic face of the latter.

This point affords a great variety of objects:—a clump of bufhes frequently relieves a piece of rock, which, as if afhamed
ed

ed to fhew itfelf, hides the greateft part
of its grandeur in a bed of mofs, or clay.
Here, as juft obferved, the commencement
of Under Cliff, towards Steep-hill, or Steeple,
as it is commonly called, takes place. And
the name of Under Cliff is not improper-
ly given to it ; as a huge precipice, of a
very confiderable height, hung fhelving on
our left-hand for many miles. In fome
places it was at leaft five hundred feet from
the level of the fea; in others not quite fo
much.

SECTION

SECTION XII.

NEAR Niton we received fo cordial and hofpitable a reception from a farmer refiding there, that to pafs it unnoticed would argue at once a want of gratitude and fenfibility.—It was one of thofe delicious moments that a heart fet in unifon with Sterne's, could alone fully enjoy—the pen of Sterne alone truly defcribe.—The power of obliging feemed to make happy; —the eyes of our kind hoft fparkled with pleafure when we partook of the refreſhment fet before us;—nor could our moft earneft entreaties prevail on him to remit his affiduities. We found in this humble fhed the plenty of a palace, without its irkfome pomp and parade.—All here was eafe, content, and happinefs.—Happy in himfelf, and happy in his connections, care had not fpread a wrinkle over the brow of our beneficent entertainer.—His countenance fpoke a heart ferene and placid, from a confcioufnefs of its own benignity. The attentive parent and the fond father

alfo

alfo betrayed itfelf in every word. " My " children," cried he, in enumerating his comforts, " I confider as one of the greateft " of the bleffings Heaven has beftowed upon " me; without them life would be infup- " portable." Speaking afterwards of his fituation, he faid, " Envy never entered " this manfion.—I covet not wealth;—the " little I have I lie down contented with, " and rife in the morning full of gratitude " to the Great Giver; nor do I know a " greater pleafure than in fharing that lit- " tle with others." As the worthy man faid this, the tear of fenfibility ftarted to his eye, and communicated to thofe of my friend, whofe hand he had fqueezed during the pious impromptu; and I could perceive a fympathetic drop fteal down his cheek alfo. " My God!" exclaimed my friend, cafting a look towards the farmer's wife and children, " this is, indeed"—Here he ftopped, and, turning, left the room. How did my heart alfo vibrate at the affecting fcene!—But to return.

Having taken leave of the worthy farmer,

mer, with every expreffion of gratitude our
lips could utter, we left his hofpitable manfion, and proceeded to Steep Hill. The af-
ternoon was, beyond defcription, enchant-
ing; the fcenes delightful ; and every thing
tended to keep alive that gentle flame of benevolent fenfibility which the foregoing incident had juft lighted up in our bofoms.

The great hand of Nature feems to have
judicioufly felected this fpot for exhibiting
one of her grandeft ftrokes. The entrance
to the cliff is from the road, which was apparently forced over rugged fteeps, that
would otherwife have been impaffable. A
grand burft broke on our left, its heights
pleafingly variegated by clinging fhrubs.
On the oppofite fide of the road lay a huge
mafs of rook that had fallen from fome
overloaded eminence, and which ferved as
a counterpart in the fore-ground. Many
others obftructed the labour of the huf-
bandman, and contributed to enrich the
fubject.

A ray of light crept imperceptibly on
the

the rocks to our left.—The effect was soft, but not equal to what a stronger light would have produced. Transits of light and shade are continually straying over these heights; which, when caught by the eye, sudden as the effect is, cannot fail to imprefs the mind with ideas of grandeur; and though the pencil might not be able to touch these transitions, the mind is not the lefs convinced of their efficacy.

For noblenefs of fore-grounds, I am of opinion, this fpot is not to be exceeded, if equalled, in England. The rocks in general are finely tinted; and lie in maffes extremely large; nor does the foliage fall fhort of its other beauties. In this part, nurtured by the foutherly winds, vegetation is moft luxuriant. A vernal-green afh, fpreading its branches to the way-worn road, is often feen entwining its charms with the ftately oak, each adding grace to the other's grandeur.

The vegetative effect which the foutherly wind has on the trees, fhrubs, and plants of this
ifland,

ifland, is worthy of remark. Long before
any of them arrive at maturity, through the
prevalence of the wind from this point, they
all incline towards the north, nodding their
ftately heads, as if they fet the chilling blafts
of Boreas at defiance. In the vallies, where
they are fheltered by the furrounding hills
from every pernicious blaft, they thrive
with an aftonifhing degree of luxuriance.—
This obfervation may feem to favour of ex-
aggeration; but fo far from it, that no defcription it is in the power of my pen to give,
can come up to the picturefque beauties thefe
fpots afford, or convey an adequate idea of
the rapturous hours I have paffed in con-
templating them.

The road to St. Lawrence is through the
fame myfterious track of rocks; but it is
kept in fuch good repair, that a carriage
may pafs with great fafety. Except here
and there a fmall clump of trees, with a
homely farm fheltering itfelf in them, nothing further worth attention ftrikes the
traveller till you approach that village.

The

The extenfion from the cliffs to the fea
fhore, is here above half a mile broad, and
poffeffed, if poffible, of far more grandeur
than thofe we had already paffed. Several
huts fkirted the road ; but we did not obferve
a houfe of any fize or confideration near it.
The church of St. Lawrence is perhaps the
fmalleft at prefent ftanding in any of the
diocefes of England ;. with a ftick of a mo-
derate length you may reach to nearly two-
thirds its height, at the weft gable end.
From the fize of the parifh, the ufual con-
gregation cannot confift of more than twenty
people, and even thofe muft fit very clofe, I
fhould imagine, to find room.

Having frequently heard of a waterfall
at this place, we had pleafed ourfelves with
the hope of feeing a grand difplay of Nature;
but were not a little furprifed to find it nothing more than the water of a fpring in the
village babbling over a few ftones.—It is almoft too inconfiderable to be noticed.

As foon as we had viewed this celebrated
waterfall, we returned to the road, and took
a view

a view of the village, which is fmall, and ftraggling. The road from Whitwell enters the cliffs here, and joins the other road in the village.—Great pains appear to have been taken to render it paffable; nor have thefe pains been unattended with fuccefs;—it exceeds the moft fanguine expectations that could have been formed of it, when firft undertaken.

There are many things in Nature which not only appear incomprehenfible to a cafual obferver, but which cannot always be accounted for by the naturalift.—Of this we met with an inftance here. We could not help furveying, with a wonder bordering on aftonifhment, the fheep that had got over the edges of the craggy precipices, from the downs they grazed on, and lay in the hollows of the rocks, in order to fhelter themfelves from the heat;—we even obferved their bleating young ones carefully to defcend, and reach their dams in fafety.— How, thus fearlefs of danger, they leave the plains, and venture on thefe hazardous declivities, where the leaft falfe ftep muft be

attended

attended with deſtruction, is, we believe,
beyond the comprehenſion of the moſt ſa-
gacious naturaliſt.—So extraordinary did it
appear to us, that nothing but ocular de-
monſtration could have convinced us of the
truth of it.—The account received from a
peaſant, had we not ſeen their ſituation,
would have met with but little credit from
us.

A phœnomenon of another nature, but
not leſs ſingular, preſented itſelf to us here.
When we ſat out from Knowle a ſtorm ſeem-
ed to be pending in the horizon; and by the
time we had reached St. Lawrence we heard
ſeveral claps of thunder.. As every incident
which tended to produce picturesque effects
inſtantly attracted our attention, we caſt our
eyes towards the ſea, in order to obſerve
whether any alteration had taken place on
its ſmooth ſurface; when, to our great ſur-
priſe, we plainly perceived a veſſel, within
eight miles of the ſhore, labouring under
the effects of the ſtorm, and apparently in
the greateſt diſtreſs. And what was extremely ſtriking was, that though the ſea
where

where the veffel happened to be, rolled (as it is commonly termed,) mountains high, yet not a breath of that air, which was there fo tempeftuous, ruffled the water on the beach beneath us.—An operation of Nature that had never before fallen under our infpection ; and we greatly regretted not having with us fome ingenious painter, in the marine line, to take an exact reprefent-ation of it.

A light, rendered more bright by the contraft, had fpread itfelf round the electric cloud, which was thus venting its rage upon the helplefs fhip, and rendered the fcene more gloomy. By a glafs, we could perceive that fhe laboured much under the violence of the ftorm, and every wave came full fraught with danger. For near an hour did the tempeft permit us to behold its raging at a. diftance ; but at length a brifk wind fpringing up, it made its way towards us, and we fhould have fhared in its " pitilefs peltings," had we not retired to a neighbouring cottage, where we continued till it had paffed on.

Having

Having returned the owner of the cottage to which we had retired, our thanks for the kind attention fhewn us, we once more mounted our horfes, and had from hence the completeft view of Undercliff, towards Bonchurch, that any part affords. The houfe of the honourable Wilbraham Tollemache appears full in fight.

The view from hence is too confufed for all the parts of it to be contracted into a landfcape; but for the fight, it has every gratification the warmeft imagination can wifh. The numbers of the rocks, and the uninterrupted verdure twining round them, with large maffes of broken ground, compofe a fcene fuperb in the extreme.

The rain, which had juft ceafed, had left its fpangles on the bladed grafs, faint imitation of the cryftal drop gently ftealing down the cheek of Beauty; and as the fofteft emotions of pity are excited in the manly breaft by thefe, fo did thofe add new charms to the verdure of the cliffs.

Vol. I.   P   Every

Every plant and fhrub was clad in its gayeft veft, and Nature feemed to be adorned with her livelieft fmiles, and to breathe forth her fweeteft fragrance.—A briar had courted the embraces of the everlafting ivy; the feafon had juft tipped their leaves with the remembrance of September, but no more than added luftre to the union. A few afhes hung vibrating from the precipice, bedecked with all the bloom that fummer could beftow upon them. While the humble thatch of the fcattered cottages, befriended by the downy mofs, glared in the brighteft yellow; which but tended to foften the mellower tints of the furrounding plants. In fhort, the fcene exhibited a profufion of charms.

To this the declining rays of the fun did not a little contribute; every fhrub or plant on which they glanced, when gently moved by the paffing zephyr, feemed to bow their heads in grateful acknowledgement to the great fource of vegetation.

The road ftill continued over the rocky
afcents

afcents of thefe chearful hills. To give an
exact reprefentation of all the fcenes we
paffed, is not in our power ;—fuffice it to
fay, that they are pleafingly irregular.—
Every hundred paces, though on fuch elevated ground, lead up a frefh hill, or elfe
fkirt the defcent with a floping flowery or-
chard.

The evening had beamed forth its laft
rays on Steep-hill Cottage, as we paffed its
elevation; and lulling all Nature to repofe,
rendered it neceffary for us to feek an afylum for the night.

P 2   SECTION

SECTION XIII.

GREAT as the pleafures were which we had enjoyed the preceding day, they did not exceed the fatisfaction we received from the permiffion granted us to view Steep-hill Cottage. This was once the villa of the late right honourable Hans Stanley, then governor of the ifland; but it now belongs to the honourable Mr. Tollemache.

It was erected by Mr. Stanley, and, from its fituation, muft have coft an immenfe fum. From feveral concurring circumftances, we were led to believe, that even bringing the water up to the houfe was attended with a very confiderable expence.

It is in the true cottage ftile.—The roof confifts, cottage like, of humble thatch; and the outfides of the walls are coyered with white compofition; forming together a rural and pleafing appearance. But its infide, for neatnefs and elegance, beggars defcription.—It is at once fo plain, fo truly elegant,

gant, and, though fmall, fo convenient, and
fo pleafant, that I think I may venture to
fay I never met with its equal.

The entrance leading from the gate to the
houfe, is lined on both fides with lofty elms
and afhes, which form an avenue that reaches
almoft to the door of the hall, where a difplay of tafte is feen in the furrounding flowers and fhrubs.

On the left hand, before we reached the
houfe, ftood an urn; and on the right hand,
a chair formed of the rough branches of
trees, which, though fimple, was curious.

As you enter the hall the fight is encountered with frefh beauties; it is not fpacious, but in the extreme of tafte.—Here are
a few pictures by Vandevelde, with feveral
by other mafters. But on entering the din-
ing room, we found an exquifite difplay of
the powers of this mafter's pencil.—We
fcarcely ever remember feeing a collection
of fhipping to be compared with it.

The

The piece in particular which hung over the fire-place, is, without exception, one of the fineſt by that maſter.—The ſubjeĉt is a ſhip in a gale of wind, under top-ſails. The handling is wonderful; and the penciling clearly pronounces it to be a *chef d'ouvre*.

Two others of conſiderable merit hung over the doors: we imagined them to be by Brooking.—They are finely touched:—the ſea, in one of them, is ſpirited to a degree. There are alſo ſome by De Velieger, executed in a fine manner, particularly the view of Scheveling.

Laſt, though not leaſt, two landſcapes attracted our notice; which, at firſt ſight, we thought to be Gainſborough's.—The colouring clear and beautiful; the drawing not leſs great; the finiſhing in his beſt ſtile.—We were however much ſurpriſed when we were informed, that they were not actually executed by that great maſter, but copied after two pieces of his, by the honourable Mr. Tollemache, the poſſeſſor of the villa.

I ſhall

I fhall not hefitate to pronounce, that were thefe pictures hanging in fome fnug corner in town, the moft experienced connoiffeur, on getting a fight of them, would immediately conclude them to be originals. They only want time to mellow their frefh appearance, and then few would be able to difcover the difference.

The fubject of one is a cottage; down the fteps of which a country girl is defcending—A favourite fubject of that eminent and much lamented mafter. The other truly depictured to us the mind of this paragon of natural genius.—It was a fmall piece of water, with a grey horfe in a market cart, fipping the furface of the pool. The diftance of both is foft and harmonious, and adds double luftre and effect to the fore-grounds. Of all the copiers from Gainfborough, no one perhaps ever caught his touch and colouring with greater exactnefs, or has been more chafte in the drawing, than Mr. Tollemache, in the pieces referred to.

There

There being company in the houfe at the time we were there, we were prevented from feeing the upper part of it ;—a difappointment we fubmitted to with regret; as from what we had feen on the ground floor, we had but little doubt of the remainder being furnifhed and decorated with equal elegance and tafte.

The outfide of the houfe is no lefs free from oftentation in its appearance, than the infide is devoid of every falfe allurement to catch the eye. The principal view from it is towards the weft; where a bow window projects, that, like the roofs of all the other parts, has only humble thatch for its covering.

A pleafing lawn lies before it, which gradually declining, prefents the whole range of St. Lawrence on one fide,—the extremity of the ocean on the other. On the right fide, at the bottom of the lawn, you pafs the wicket that leads to the garden, which, from its fituation, cannot fail of being productive. The rocks protect

it

it towards the north, and the fea breezes fan it from the fouth.

From hence we paffed the wing of the houfe, and entered a path that leads to the grove before mentioned. The offices are fome of them in the village, others are adjoining to the houfe. On the left hand ftands the green-houfe and ftabling, but they lie confiderably lower than the cottage.

To enumerate the many delightful viciffitudes of this fairy ground, is beyond the power of a pen. I therefore fhall conclude my defcription of it with faying, that to find a fpot where thofe who refide in it are fo much refpected,—where its vicinity is fo pleafing,—its fituation fo romantic,—and its *tout en-femble* fo bewitching,—is next to impoffible.

Mr. Tollemache has likewife a brigantine yacht, which, when the weather will permit, lies here to grace the ruder fcenes of Nature. The infide of it, we were informed,

is

is equally as elegant as his villa, and fitted up with the fame tafte; but we had not an opportunity of viewing it.

Parties frequently come to the New Inn, at Steephill, to dine ; where, though they might not find the fumptuous entertainment of a modern hotel, they will meet with every convenience for ferving up a cold collation.

· Even in this reclufe and humble fituation a ray of tafte is vifible. The houfe being fmall, the proprietors have encouraged the irregular branches of a fig tree to repofe itfelf on an artificial fupport ; thereby forming a kind of canopy, which fpreading over a daifey-mantled carpet, ferves as a pleafing and agreeable receptacle, in which parties continually dine, *al frefco*. On the oppofite fide a prouder walnut fpreads its branches over the feats, and likewife fhelters the chearful guefts from the fcorching beams of the fun.

The profpect from thefe rural fheds is very pleafing, but, in point of landfcape,

rather

rather contracted. The hill from whence the village derives its name binds the left-hand fcreen. The valley opens beneath to the road where Mr. Tollemache's yacht ufually lies. To fhew how much we were charmed with this place, I cannot help making ufe of an expreffion of the late Mr. Quin's, on his leaving Chatfworth: "I thought I fhould at times have broke my neck in getting there; but when I was there, I thought I fhould have broke my heart to leave it."

The fhore here is very rocky, and, when the wind blows frefh from the fouthward, very dangerous for fhips. At fuch times the yacht leaves her ftation, and makes for Sandown Bay, or for Spithead.

The inhabitants fay, that within the laft twenty years the fea has greatly incroached, at this part of the coaft, on the land. But if we might judge from the pieces of rock with which the ftrand is every where ftrewed, and which muft have fallen from the eminences at the time the fea wafhed their fides, (and this, from every apparent circumftance,

cumftance, muft have been the cafe at fome period or other,) it may rather, I think, be concluded that the contrary has happened. The country people, however, think otherwife.

A number of ravens build in thefe cliffs, and likewife hawks, of a fpecies peculiar to this fpot only;—they are of the falcon kind, and found to be the only fort proper for the fport of hawking. Jack-daws, crows, and many other birds, alfo make them their habitations, and breed on them. Some of the farmers fay they have heard of eagles being there; others are of a different opinion. From the fituation of the rocks, fuch a circumftance is not improbable; but as this bird is generally an inhabitant of colder climates, we were rather inclined to give credit to the affertions of the latter.

The people of this place are chiefly fifhermen, who in the fummer feafon take great quantities of crabs and lobfters. For this purpofe fome of them fink more than

a hundred

a hundred wicker pots, or more properly baſkets, at a time; which they bait with whatever kind of fleſh or garbage they can procure. And here it may not be improper to hint to the gentlemen of the iſland, that whenever they loſe a dog, they cannot ſeek for it in a more likely place; though moſt probably they may chance to come too late to recover it while living. I have myſelf ſeen ſeveral fine pointers tied up in their huts at a night, which, before the ſucceeding day has broke, have been made not " worms meat," as Mercutio was, but food for crabs and lobſters. The coaſt abounds with ſhell fiſh of all ſorts, to the great convenience of the lower ranks, who purchaſe them at three pence per pound; that is generally the price fixed when boiled, and they are always ſold by weight.

A fiſh of a very peculiar nature is ſome- times taken here, to which the fiſhermen, from its circular form, give the name of the ſun-fiſh. The appearance of this fiſh is extremely whimſical, and Nature ſeems to have been in a ſportive humour when ſhe

she first fashioned it. In shape it is nearly round, and does not, like most other fish, branch out into any part that might be termed a tail. One part however is rather pointed, at which the head is fixed; the shoulders are placed at the thickest part; after which it becomes rather oval; and it has four fins, situated at the extremities. Taken altogether, it is a droll composition. We could not help resembling it to a school-boy, who, having worn his long hair for a considerable time dangling down his back, has it, on a sudden, cropped close to his neck.

We had been informed, that here, also, we should see a cascade; our expectations however were soon put a stop to, by beholding a little spring, trickling down the side of a hill, in a contracted channel, devoid of every appearance of grandeur; and possessing nothing worthy of notice, but the large stone by which its mean clue was broken, and which was sufficient to sustain a body of water fifty times more weighty than that running over it.

Leaving

Leaving Steephill, we continued our
courfe towards Bonchurch; during which
feveral curious ftudies for colouring prefented themfelves, till we paffed the corner of a
precipice, from whence the beginning of
Little-town Down commences. The fhelving fides of this precipice hang tottering
over the brink of the deep abyfs, and threat-
en an intrufion on the road.—It forms a
noble fide-fcreen for the general view of
Bonchurch;—while from it the fea has a
variegated appearance, and finely affifts the
landfcape.

On firft viewing the mountain to which
the name of Little-town Down is given, a
traveller may be led to fuppofe it Steep-
hill. Its fides, like that, are almoft perpendicular, and, as feen from the road, are
formed like a fugar-loaf. A few houfes lie
at its foot; the road to which from Appuldurcombe is dangerous in the extreme. The
hill itfelf is a noble picturefque object; and
forms an elegant back-ground to relieve the
broken part of the road on which the cottages ftand. Here are as many choice
pieces

pieces of broken rocks, and fore-grounds well verdured, as at Undercliff; only more contrasted. The soil again alters here, and appears to be composed of flint, with great quantities of tobacco-pipe clay.

END OF THE FIRST VOLUME.

Ingram Content Group UK Ltd.
Milton Keynes UK
UKHW031502090323
418300UK00009B/832